Buy Gold and Silver Safely

by

Doug Eberhardt

© Copyright 2018, Doug Eberhardt

All Rights Reserved.

No part of this book may be reproduced, stored in a retrieval system, or transmitted by any means, electronic, mechanical, photocopying, recording, or otherwise, without written permission from the author.

ISBN: **978-0-9825861-7-4**

Dedicated to Chris Furman for all you do.

The most important aspect to learning about buying gold and silver is to know what you are doing and what you want to buy before calling a gold dealer. This is why I wrote the book; so you don't make any mistakes.

Enjoy the book!

DISCLAIMER

EVERY EFFORT HAS BEEN MADE TO ACCURATELY REPRESENT THIS PRODUCT AND SERVICES OFFERED, AND ITS POTENTIAL. THERE IS NO GUARANTEE THAT YOU WILL EARN ANY MONEY USING THE TECHNIQUES AND IDEAS IN THIS BOOK. EXAMPLES IN THE BOOK ARE NOT TO BE INTERPRETED AS A PROMISE OR GUARANTEE OF EARNINGS. EARNING POTENTIAL IS ENTIRELY DEPENDENT ON THE PERSON USING THE INFORMATION INCLUDED TO THE BOOK AND THE IDEAS AND THE TECHNIQUES. WE DO NOT PURPORT THIS AS A GET RICH SCHEME. YOUR LEVEL OF SUCCESS IN ATTAINING THE RESULTS IN THIS BOOK DEPENDS ON THE TIME YOU DEVOTE TO THE IDEAS AND TECHNIQUES MENTIONED, YOUR FINANCES, KNOWLEDGE AND VARIOUS SKILLS. SINCE THESE FACTORS DIFFER ACCORDING TO INDIVIDUALS, WE CANNOT GUARANTEE YOUR SUCCESS OR PROFIT LEVEL. NOR ARE WE RESPONSIBLE FOR ANY OF YOUR ACTIONS. MATERIALS IN THIS BOOK MAY CONTAIN INFORMATION THAT INCLUDES FORWARD-LOOKING STATEMENTS THAT GIVE OUR EXPECTATIONS OR FORECASTS OF FUTURE EVENTS. YOU CAN IDENTIFY THESE STATEMENTS BY THE FACT THAT THEY DO NOT RELATE STRICTLY TO HISTORICAL OR CURRENT FACTS. THEY USE WORDS SUCH AS ANTICIPATE, ESTIMATE, EXPECT, PROJECT, INTEND, PLAN, BELIEVE, AND OTHER WORDS AND TERMS OF SIMILAR MEANING IN CONNECTION WITH A DESCRIPTION OF POTENTIAL EARNINGS OR FINANCIAL PERFORMANCE. ANY AND ALL FORWARD-LOOKING STATEMENTS IN THIS BOOK ARE INTENDED TO EXPRESS OUR OPINION OF EARNINGS POTENTIAL. MANY FACTORS WILL BE IMPORTANT IN DETERMINING YOUR ACTUAL RESULTS AND NO GUARANTEES ARE MADE THAT YOU WILL ACHIEVE RESULTS SIMILAR TO OURS OR ANYBODY ELSE'S, IN FACT NO GUARANTEES ARE MADE THAT YOU WILL ACHIEVE ANY RESULTS FROM OUR IDEAS AND TECHNIQUES IN OUR MATERIALS AT ALL.

TABLE OF CONTENTS

Introduction xi

PART I - GOLD 1

Chapter 1	"What Backs the U.S. Dollar?" 3
Chapter 2	A Brief History of Gold and Federal Reserve Notes 22
Chapter 3	Flaws of the Financial Services Industry 31
Chapter 4	How a Deflationary Contraction Unfolds 40
Chapter 5	Common Objections to Buying Gold 81
Chapter 6	How Does Gold Fit Into A Diversified Portfolio? 86
Chapter 7	Types of Gold Investments 99
Chapter 8	Who Is Recommending Gold and Why? 118
Chapter 9	Physical Gold - A Must For Every Portfolio and Gold Investment Grid 132
Chapter 10	How Do You Store Your Gold? 139
Chapter 11	Places To Purchase Physical Gold 144
Chapter 12	Investing in Gold With an IRA or 401(k) 147
Chapter 13	Where To Sell Gold 152

PART II - SILVER 154

Chapter 14	Silver: The Other Precious Metal 155
Chapter 15	Silver Uses, Supply and Demand 161
Chapter 16	Silver Is Money Today 169
Chapter 17	Gold/Silver Ratios 173
Chapter 18	Types of Silver to Invest In 175
Chapter 19	How to Profit By Investing in Silver 179

Conclusion 184
Glossary 189
Index 195

Introduction

Where does gold fit into a diversified investment? People have worked hard to accumulate wealth and can't afford to make mistakes that would cause them to lose on their investments. All they want is some peace of mind with their investments moving forward; confident they are making the best investment decisions. Reading a book about investing in gold won't give you all the answers you need on where to invest and that is why I wrote a second book called Illusions of Wealth which you can find on Amazon.com. That book is a reference guide for new or old investors, something you can refer back to time and time again on investment strategies.

This book is the updated second version of the first book Buy Gold and Silver Safely first written in 2010. Times change and the investment climate changes with it along with monetary and political decisions which means the information about gold needs to be updated from time to time. But two things that don't change are accumulated National Debt and gold. An ounce of gold is always an ounce of gold, but government always adds to the National Debt and the paper money called dollars will buy you less and less over time (also known as inflation).

The advice investors relied on in the past didn't protect them from the 2008/2009 market decline. After that episode the stock market skyrocketed. President Barack Obama during his Presidential campaign called then current President George W. Bush "unpatriotic" for raising the debt limit from $4 trillion to $8 trillion. While in office, President Obama raised the national debt by $9 trillion. Some might question how patriotic that was, but this isn't a political book, although politicians on both sides are responsible for today's debt which is now north of $20 Trillion. It is a disease perpetrated on us by congress that is out of control and can spread economic havoc at some point in the future. What President Trump or any future President can do is unknown, but can we really expect austerity? What insurance do you have to counter this potential monetary disaster when interest rates increase the interest on the debt to where Congress can't help but inflate away their problems by printing even more money?

That insurance is gold.

Today people find themselves having recovered from one market decline but always asking, "is the next collapse around the corner?" Can my portfolio afford to experience another decline like we had in 2008/2009?

Financial advisors were never taught the significance of gold and silver in one's portfolio. It's no wonder, as the entire financial and educational systems are biased against gold and silver. I have even heard CNBC commentators ask the question; "What is gold?" But I also based this analysis on the books provided to Certified Financial Planners (CFP) candidates and the complicity of the media, government and Federal Reserve, who all want you to believe in a system that is flawed at its core because governments don't stop spending but granted it has worked since 1971 when we went of the gold standard. Thinking about it another way, if President Bush throws $4 trillion into the economy and President Obama $9 trillion, there can be and has been some good that came out of it. But at what expense. For every action there is a reaction. And if you spend more money that what you have your credit card companies stop giving you credit. So what could go wrong with government spending more money than what they have? How long can they print money before everyone realizes that our money is not keeping up with the prices of things? How many of you even know what a super inflation can do to your portfolio? You don't unless you lived in the 70's. We've had quite a ride the last 40/50 year, but it won't last.

But here is the key that most don't understand about money and inflation. We here in the U.S. have a central bank called the Federal Reserve that has as a mandate to have 2% inflation. This means they want the price of things to go up by 2% a year. Your dollars have to grow by 2% a year to keep pace with this goal. In the 1970's, after Nixon took us off the gold standard, dollars couldn't keep up with inflation, but gold did. The crazy part about this mandate though is in

10 years you must pay 20% more for things than today if they maintain their mandate. Why would anyone want to do that? The answer is so the Federal Reserve System works to benefit them, not you. It's how our whole monetary system works which you'll learn later in this book and how gold can counteract their monetary mayhem policies of inflation targeting.

Our financial system is based on blind faith in a piece of paper that has 46 short years of existence without a relationship to gold. Let that sink in for a moment.

All Central Banks in the world hold gold to give the illusion that the currencies they print are backed by gold. If all Central Banks hold gold, why is it mocked by CNBC as "just a shiny rock?"

CNBC commentators can't even get that last statement straight, as gold isn't even a rock, but a metal; a "precious" metal with over 5,000 years of history being utilized as money all over the world. The same can be said of silver, as it has a similar history as money.

This may come as a shock to most gold bugs out there; gold **is** just a shiny metal. That's right, bury it in your backyard 10 years ago, dig it up today, clean it up, and it's still a shiny metal. But that metal is worth much more today as it was 10 years ago. Why? Because it's what the shiny metal is priced in—U.S. dollars—that matters.

It is only the value of the U.S. dollar that has changed. Gold didn't change. A higher gold price exposes the weakness of the dollar, or the lack of belief in the future of the dollar's purchasing power.

The weakness or strength of the dollar relies solely on the collective views of the crowd. At one time the crowd believed tulips were as good or better than gold. Then the bottom fell out. Some in that crowd think Bitcoin can go to 100,000 or more. But bitcoins for the most part, cannot act as money, are typically illiquid and way to volatile for most investors. However, there is merit here. I'll explain more through a company called Goldmoney Inc. (Symbol TSX: XAU) that is listed on the Toronto Stock Exchange and allows you to invest in and transact in both physical gold/silver and some cryptocurrencies. First of its kind.

Even if this book convinces you to buy gold, you still are in danger of not knowing what to buy. The gold market is filled with sharks and charlatans who are out to rip you off. You see their ads on television and hear them on the radio or find them through searches on the internet where they manipulate Google's algorithms to be in the top 10 searches, so you'll click their link or pay a ton for adds on searches for "buy gold" and what not. Investors need to take some responsibility for their financial future and get educated on gold and silver before diving in. Naturally, this book, *Buy Gold and Silver Safely*, provides answers by explaining why gold and silver need to be a part of everyone's portfolio and helping people learn about buying the right gold and silver products and avoid the high commission that unscrupulous dealers charge, taking advantage of those who know very little about buying precious metals.

If everyone read this book, these companies would simply go out of business. That's my goal in writing this book, to stomp out those who try to rip you off and get investors to buy the low commissioned gold that can see profits grow for them, not the gold dealer. But first, we'll discuss why gold needs to be a part of your portfolio.

PART I - GOLD

CHAPTER 1
"What Backs the U.S. Dollar?

What happens when the stimulus-spending Congress and the Federal Reserve are dishing out starts to hit the purchasing power of the dollar negatively? Why is there so much faith in the dollar? What really backs the U.S. dollar? This is a good place to start the conversation and see where gold fits in.

What Backs the U.S. Dollar?

If you Google the phrase "What backs the U.S. Dollar?" you come to what Google has chosen as the best answer from an article I wrote, and no, I didn't pay some SEO company to get my article as the best answer.

It really took some digging to get to the real answer to this question, and we have the U.S. government's own words to help us.

In 1971, the U.S. decided to go it alone without our money tied to gold because other countries were requesting our gold in payment instead of Federal Reserve Notes (dollars). President Nixon removed the U.S. dollar from any ties to gold and basically was the equivalent of telling the rest of the world to take our paper dollars or you get nothing. This is where the saying "U.S. dollars are backed by the full faith and credit of the U.S. Government" comes from.

The U.S. just before this time was a world superpower, having been victorious in WWII. There really wasn't anything other countries could do about the decision by the U.S. government to abandon metal backing. Subsequently, the rest of the world followed suit as it fit right in with what Central Banks wanted to do, keep countries in perpetual debt as they collect the interest.

What does a U.S. dollar, or "Federal Reserve Note" (FRN) as it is known, represent now that gold and silver no longer back any of the currency printed in the U.S.?

A $10 bill used say on it, "Redeemable in Gold Coin." Once President Roosevelt in 1934 severed the tie of FRN's and gold, the

FRN's now said on them; "This note is legal tender for all debts, public and private, and is redeemable in lawful money at the United States Treasury or at any Federal Reserve Bank." But what is "lawful money?" It was assumed then that lawful money was gold. Look at a dollar bill today. It simply says; "This note is legal tender for all debts, public and private." In other words, you can't even redeem it for "lawful money" any longer. A dollar bill is not lawful money, but rather "legal tender."[1]

From the Treasury:

> **"Federal Reserve notes are not redeemable in gold, silver or any other commodity, and receive no backing by anything.** Redeemable notes into gold ended in 1933 and silver in 1968. **The notes have no value for themselves**, but for what they will buy. In another sense, because they are legal tender, Federal Reserve notes are 'backed' by all the goods and services in the economy."[2] (emphasis added)

What the government, via the Treasury and the Federal Reserve, really did was coerce you to accept something—FRNs—that used to be redeemable for gold and/or silver, but now aren't redeemable at all.

Let's play along with the Treasury's definition of FRNs and see if "all the goods and services in the economy" really do back the U.S. dollar.

What the Treasury would have you believe is that GDP backs the dollar. GDP is defined as "the monetary value of all finished goods and services within a country's borders in a specific time period. It includes all private and public consumption, government outlays, investments and exports less imports that occur within a defined territory."[3]

To break it down:

---

[1] U.S. Treasury FAQ; Legal Tender Status
http://www.ustreas.gov/education/faq/currency/legal-tender.shtml
[2] ibid – emphasis added
[3] Gross Domestic Product – Farlex Financial Dictionary
http://financial-dictionary.thefreedictionary.com/Per+capita+GDP

$$GDP = C + I + NX + G$$

Where:
"C" is equal to all private consumption, or consumer spending, in a nation's economy
"I" is the sum of all the country's businesses spending on capital
"NX" is the nation's total net exports, calculated as total exports minus total imports. (NX = Exports – Imports)
"G" is the sum of government spending

Consumer spending is what drives an economy and is said to be responsible for 70% of its growth. But no offense to any readers, but consumers aren't typically overall too smart with their money, so they go into debt and will spend till the debt load is too much and subsequently this reduced spending causes a contraction in the economy. This contraction affects business spending too as it decreases with less consumers wanting things. So, what's left to drive the economy? I refer you to the "unpatriotic" government spending from 2004 to 2018 I referenced in the introduction of this book where we saw the national debt grow from $4 trillion to over $20 trillion as this spending supplemented what consumers and business couldn't provide (because they live within their means).

In 2017 we saw that President Trump wanted to add at least $1 trillion more to the national debt through various non-income producing infrastructure spending and increases in the military budget all the while reducing corporate and personal income taxes with tax reform that passed. Trump has said that he wants to borrow more now while interest rates are lower because we won't be able to borrow when interest rates are higher. Little does he understand that the borrowing we do today will have a higher cost when interest rates move higher as the interest taxpayers have to pay on the debt will be greater. But let's not kid ourselves. It's our children and their children and on down the line who will bear this burden. This is what happens when monetary policy is left on its own without a relationship to gold. But how will it end?

Government Spending Is All That Is Running the Show

Many don't even realize it, but government spending is all that is running the show. It's been that way basically since the Presidency of Ronald Reagan and his increase in the military budget. As much as Reagan is admired for many good reasons, no one seems to understand that many of the good times we have had since was this change in the way government runs things with a checkbook that has no limits to the amount it can write on it. Sure, they do every so often come out with a balanced budget, but there has not been one that has worked as planned. This is the nature of the beast known as leviathan for you Biblically minded out there.

Let me pose a question to you; Does it work out well for the individual who obtains more credit cards and immediately uses this newly created credit to pay for old debt? At the same time the temptation of new found money (credit) gives the one with it the temptation to buy more "things" while trying to maintain payments for their current expenses. The result of this added credit for the consumer is it increases the monthly amount of interest one must pay in servicing the debt because the amount of debt increases. At some point, more credit cards will be needed if the individual's income stays the same, or the possibility of missing payments and default surfaces. If the consumer can't borrow more, what choices do they have? The U.S. government however does not worry about this need for extra income to pay their bills. Congress simply votes to continually increase the National Debt limit. President Trump in 2017 even went so far to say "why have a debt ceiling?"[4]

So how will this increase in spending work for the U.S. government? It can work well if everyone believes in the monetary

---

[4] "...why have a debt ceiling?" – Remarks by Donald Trump
http://www.politico.com/story/2017/09/07/trump-end-debt-ceiling-votes-242429

unit (FRN's) that are being printed out of thin air. Technically speaking though, it's the borrowing of more money from the treasury, not actually printing dollars.

If the extra government spending to stimulate the economy goes into government jobs, do people even realize this is not creating growth? Creating a government job is increasing the debt by the salary given to the government employee but doesn't necessarily equate to production increases.

If this theory of GDP backing the dollar is viable, and if government spending is all that is backing the dollar at this point in time, how is this money repaid?

The answer can only be from U.S. citizens, through higher taxes or the hidden tax of inflation.

Since politicians don't get elected by raising taxes, that leaves only two viable answers; printing it, or the tool of choice for the Federal Reserve, borrowing from the Japanese or Chinese through the sale of Treasuries.

It's a nice legacy that our generation is leaving future generations, isn't it?

You load sixteen tons, what do you get
Another day older and deeper in debt
Saint Peter don't you call me 'cause I can't go
I owe my soul to the company store

—Tennessee Ernie Ford

The Madness of Government Spending

The George W. Bush administration's spending was out-of-control and President Barack Obama's administration was doubling the amount of debt. President Trump is also increasing debt. You see, it doesn't matter if it is a Republican or Democrat President or even who controls Congress. They vote to increase the debt limit each and every time. Both sides will drive this nation into a black hole of financial debt as far as the eye can see. Congress continues to raise the debt ceiling, which is now over $20 trillion. What these bureaucrats fail to realize is they have it backwards compared to the individual who obtains more credit. They have no consequences to their spending habits. But it is the People of the United States who will bear the burden at some point for their choices. The system will collapse as long as government keeps spending. But I guess the government failed that math class, didn't they? A consumer may be able to declare bankruptcy to get a fresh start, but what can a government do?

If you want to put this government spending into perspective, please take the time now and watch a video put out by DebtLimitUSA called It's A Bank.

https://www.youtube.com/watch?v=Li0no7O9zmE

They don't update it every year like I wish they would, but the humor in it cracks me up to this day, as sad as the situation really is for future generations in the U.S.

The reality with this government spending theory of GDP backing the dollar though is flawed to begin with. The dollar acts as a medium of exchange and is only considered valuable because it can be exchanged for goods and services. **It is one's production that is actually backing the dollar.**

When one looks at a dollar bill they'll notice it says the following at the top: "Federal Reserve Note."

What is the legal definition of "Federal Reserve Note?"

A Federal Note is defined as:

> "A Federal Reserve Note is the paper currency in circulation in the United States. Federal Reserve Notes are a kind of United States banknote printed by the United States Bureau of Engraving and Printing. Section 411 of Title 12 of the United States Code authorizes a Federal Reserve Note. Pursuant to the Federal Reserve Act of 1913, the Federal Reserve Banks issue these notes and are effectively non-interest-bearing promissory notes payable to bearer on demand. Federal Reserve Notes are issued in denominations of $1, $2, $5, $10, $20, $50, $100, $500, $1,000, $5,000, and $10,000. These

notes bear the words "this note is legal tender for all debts, public and private."[5]

I thought one's production via their labor was something they got to keep? But according to how they are being paid for their labor, i.e. in dollars, they are accepting IOUs instead. An IOU that is forever buying them less and less!

People cannot collect on those IOUs until they are exchanged for something of value. Even if one puts them in CDs, money markets and U.S. Treasuries, they only represent an IOU promise of FRNs in the future. What those FRNs can be exchanged for down the road will have less purchasing power than it does today and always will as long as we have inflation.

But what will Japan and China exchange their Treasuries for in the future and when will they unload them? This is a question no one in Congress dares to ask, but you should ponder it seriously if you want to protect your own purchasing power. In January 2018 China did make a threat to just slow or halt purchases of U.S. treasuries and the dollar plummeted 2 points. Imagine what would happen if they started selling? Same with Japan. This is the area your portfolio is typically lacking the insurance gold provides if a dollar fall is on the horizon.[6]

Since people can't redeem these IOUs for "lawful" money (gold or silver) any longer, what makes them think that these pieces of paper called "notes" that have less than 50 years of existence without gold or silver backing, are going to maintain their purchasing power in the years to come? Have they in the last 50 years? The good news is, some of them can be exchanged for gold and silver today. You do that through a gold dealer. However there needs to be caution in doing so which we'll show in Chapter 8 because not all gold dealers have your best interest at heart.

---

[5] Federal Reserve Note Law & Legal Definition
http://definitions.uslegal.com/f/federal-reserve-note/
[6] https://www.bloomberg.com/news/articles/2018-01-10/china-officials-are-said-to-view-treasuries-as-less-attractive

Now you know what backs the dollar, but when financial media talks about a strong or weak dollar, what are they really saying? This is where most people, including many on Wall Street, don't have a clue.

The Dollar Index

The dollar they talk about in financial media is really the Dollar Index. The Dollar Index is computed using a trade-weighted average of the following six currencies:

Euro	57.6 %
Japan/Yen	13.6 %
UK/Pound	11.9 %
Canada/Dollar	9.1 %
Sweden/Krona	4.2 %
Switzerland/Franc	3.6 %

The dollar then is really **valued** based on what these currencies do.

The index was introduced in 1973 with a base of 100 and incorporated the Euro when it was introduced in 1999. To answer the question then, what is a dollar? – we answer by saying it is a representation of these 6 currencies with over half the value of the dollar represented by the Euro. In essence, if the Euro falls in value, the dollar rises and vice versa.

Can the Dollar Crash?

We hear many gold bugs continually say year after year the dollar is going to crash. They say this because of the massive amount of debt the U.S. has on the books. But why with the over $20 trillion of additional National Debt has the dollar maintained its value for the most part? Gold bugs can't typically answer that because they don't understand the dollar can't crash. If it did, by default the Euro, Yen, Pound and the other currencies that represent what a dollar is would have to skyrocket. This is how currencies work and something that most in the financial media don't understand. This is part of the illusion of what a dollar truly represents.

The dollar is on one side of the ship, and the other currencies on the other side. They move back and forth, higher and lower over time when they are priced in each other but can never literally crash or sink the ship. However, as the debt of all these nations pile up that make up these currencies increases, it is the eventuality of higher rates that will crash them all and the only life boats will be made of gold. **Gold maintains its purchasing power over time, not fiat currencies.** Emphasis in "over time" for you naysayers out there. Anyone can pick a point in time the last 50 years and make a case for or against gold or the dollar. There are times when each has value. But only one has over $20 trillion of debt backing it and a complicit government in increasing that debt year after year after year (both parties).

Pricing currencies in each other when each currency itself has a very high Debt to GDP ratio backing it, with no austerity to decrease the debt, means that GDP won't keep up and an economy crashes. What comes next is inflation and super inflation and the possibility of hyperinflation. It's a recipe for disaster. But what will trigger it? How have we got away with this unbelievable amount of debt increase this long? How can a nation that has over $20 trillion of debt, more than the entire S&P stock market value, maintain purchasing power?

It shouldn't. But this is the elephant in the room for all nations we're just supposed to ignore. The old saying; "move along, there's nothing to see here" is what we're dealing with. Or "don't pay attention to the man behind the curtain." That "man" is the Federal Reserve but also Congress that does a good job in pulling the wool over investor's eyes as FRN's maintain their value. For how long, remains to be seen.

The following chart highlights just how far the Dollar Index fell, resulting in a bottom of just under 72 in March of 2008. During this time gold skyrocketed higher and the bottoming of the Index coincided with a new high of gold.

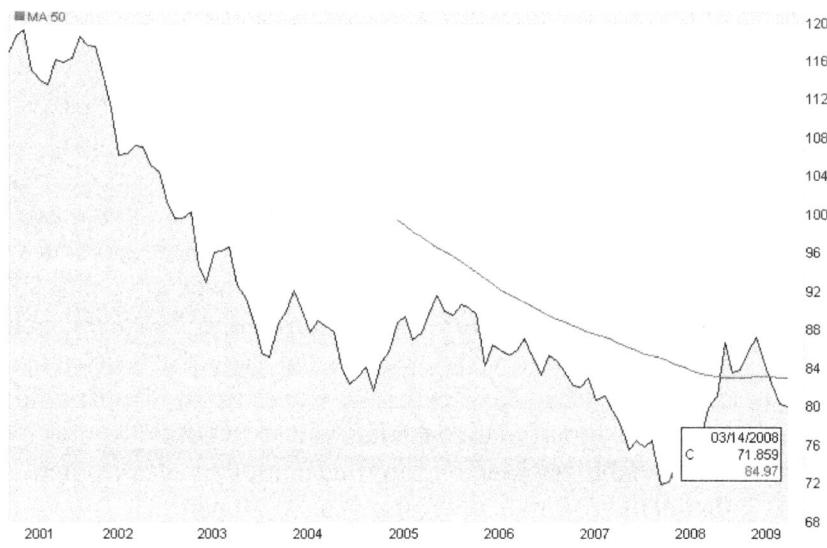

As you can see, the dollar was in a secular bear market since the year 2000 versus this basket of currencies and is in the process of an overall rebound since the 2008 low and the onset of the financial crisis.

But what happens next? Where is the dollar going and where is gold going? The dollar has a good chance of heading up to 120 again in a true deflationary credit contraction (See Chapter 4), putting pressure on gold for a bit, but this pressure will be short lived. I spend every week calling the ups and downs of the gold market with my writing and I can distinguish the micro moves versus macro moves based on my analysis. One thing I can state for certain no matter what the current view of the markets and gold may be, up or down, the future for gold is bright and there is a good reason why I am choosing this point in time to update this book. Your awareness of what is potentially on the horizon is paramount to your overall strategy of wealth preservation and insurance for what may come.

The Fed, Treasury and Congress can only choose to inflate away their future problems in paying off this debt. To do this they will need to somehow lower the value of the dollar. They will be using inflated dollars to pay off old debt.

But the Fed doesn't necessarily get it right. Former Fed Chairman Ben Bernanke gave us some insight as to what he would do to stimulate the economy in a 2002 speech. He said he would fight any deflation by not adhering to the policy mistakes that he claims were made during the Great Depression.[7] In other words, he will inflate, inflate, inflate. "Inflate or die," as veteran market analyst and Dow Theorist Richard Russell used to say over and over before his passing in 2015.

But flash forward to 2017 and as much Quantitative Easing (QE) the Fed implemented, the Fed couldn't get inflation to 2%. This according to then Fed Chairman Janet Yellen, was a "mystery."[8]

The Fed and Congress have only three policy options should things become worrisome for the economy:

1. More Quantitative Easing; The Fed has done a decent job of maintain stability of the financial markets and prices by keeping interest rates artificially low and bailing out troubled institutions along with various bouts of increased liquidity through QE.

    Since interest rates are already low, there isn't much room to flood the system with more money. Fed Chairman Ben Bernanke says the mistake made in the Great Depression era was that there wasn't enough liquidity supplied by the Fed.

---

[7] Deflation: Making Sure "It" Doesn't Happen Here - Remarks by Governor Ben S. Bernanke
http://www.federalreserve.gov/boardDocs/speeches/2002/20021121/default.htm

[8] Remarks by Fed Chairperson Janet Yellen
https://www.bloomberg.com/news/articles/2017-09-20/yellen-brushes-aside-inflation-mystery-as-fed-eyes-rate-hike

Central banks are not going to make the same mistake Bernanke claims was made in the 1930s. But without real growth, the Fed cannot afford to raise interest rates too much, but in 2017 and 2018 they did despite underperforming GDP. For if they are raising rates too fast, any chance of an economic recovery is stopped dead in its tracks. That's what we're going to see occur I think in 2018.

Higher interest rates would bring an economic contraction, where people would find it more difficult to obtain loans for buying homes and businesses would find no capital to expand. The result of any further interference in the markets should the Fed implement more money printing or QE is it could develop into a recession, depression and possible hyperinflation if the Fed decides to keep giving the economy more of the same printing-press medicine. This, unfortunately, is all they know how to do.

Does giving a drunk another drink cure their alcoholism? Is the prescription for getting a heroin addict off the drug to give them more heroin? Does pouring more gasoline on a fire put out the fire? Does our government understand simple analogies? No. They only know how to do what has worked with no repercussions; spend and print.

The reality is, there is a subliminal contraction already occurring as any inflation is being dwarfed by the credit contraction that is occurring. In a sense, we are seeing monetary inflation within a larger credit contraction or deflation. Bernanke's speech was about using the "printing press" to fight deflation. But you'll see in Chapter 4, why this won't work.

2. Default – This is the other option and is not one the Fed is considering or would consider as it would put them out of business. Default sure would be appropriate for all the youth of the day and future generations, but they don't get to choose this. A fresh start for them would be great as there won't be a lot of pain, but it wouldn't be fair to all those who have paid into a pension and social security system shooting off streams

of income that rely on a stable dollar's value to survive. The government can't simply walk away from the debt by declaring bankruptcy and receive a fresh start. And the People of the United States must do their own thinking on how to get through the coming monetary crisis if the government doesn't get its act together.

Sure, this option would have a devastating effect on the economy, but at least there would be a fresh start to build a new system. Instead, all we are doing is stealing from future generations by pretending that things will take care of themselves through future growth of GDP. The media is complicit as they play the game of diversion with the topic du jour that keeps our minds busy arguing left versus right issues when the government (emperor) has no clothes. Again, I am treading here on a political book We the Serfs! that should be out soon if not already out as you are reading this.

When you see the Fed start buying their own Treasuries from China and Japan, inflation will be just around the corner. Gold and silver provide the peace of mind one will need whenever that day arrives. In a sense, the Fed isn't the lender of last resort as they have been known to be, but the "buyer" of last resort.

How Does Investing in Gold Relate to Your Retirement Planning?

In this opening chapter I wanted to touch on what backs the U.S. dollar (FRN's), GDP, Congressional spending, the Federal Reserve, the banking system and a little bit on inflation, credit contraction and deflation. This chapter sets the tone for the rest of the book, where I present the case for diversifying one's portfolio with the addition of physical gold and silver. And please know that throughout this book when I use the term "gold" that it also includes silver, but I don't want to have to write "gold and silver" each time. Silver has its own benefits which we'll discuss in the Silver section later in this book.

An important issue from the beginning though is that this analysis would be incomplete if I didn't also address the financial services industry and their treatment of gold.

Today, most people in the U.S. don't understand how gold fits into one's portfolio. The reason is most financial advisors don't understand much about gold as none of us were ever taught anything about it in our continued education. We're taught other philosophies and I'll address some of them as to why gold is the forgotten metal. Then later in the book I take the discussion deeper, as I critique Modern Portfolio Theory and the Prudent Man Rule, two investment theories that current financial advice is based upon, and expose their flaws, especially when they are based on what backs the entire system; Federal Reserve Notes and Treasuries.

While this book is about how to buy gold and silver safely, I thought it important for people to first understand what's really going on in the economy and to discern for themselves whether the advice one receives from their advisors, whomever they may be, is based on today's reality.

The reason I say, "whomever they may be" when referring to advisors is that most people buy investments because they trust the person sitting across the desk from them. If they don't trust the person doing the advising, they simply don't buy. That's why most advisors are prepared well in advance, before even seeing a prospect, to handle all the objections they may throw at them. Their goal is not as much to sell people an investment that makes sense for them—although many I'm sure have good intent of doing so—as is it is to get people to like them. If they like the advisor and trust them, then they'll buy from them. It's as simple as that.

The psychology of buying goes beyond the obvious. Advisors can be taught how to get you to like them through various subliminal techniques and can control conversations by using language patterns a certain way. There's a whole science called Neuro-Linguistic Programming that has a sect dedicated to these techniques. I know, because I went through the training myself.

It is these techniques that advisors use in transferring your money from where it's currently parked and getting you to put it with their recommended investment.

Gold-dealers are adept at doing this as well. They also use fear to get someone to invest. Since most people really don't know anything about gold to begin with, they become easy prey for the gold-dealer tactics to buy gold but then are sold the type of gold (or silver) that has a high commission associated with it. I know this, too, since I worked for one of these gold dealers. I know all their secrets and try to expose them as much as I can. I expose the gold-dealer's tactics later in the book in Chapter 8 so you don't make the wrong choices.

But first, while some may already be convinced of the need to buy gold and silver, others need to know the reasons why they should have some gold and silver exposure in their portfolio. The next few chapters provide a convincing argument for gold and silver.

I begin the discussion with a critique of the typical asset allocations recommended by most advisors and investment companies today as there is a certain type of risk that goes unaddressed by them that you need to be aware of.

Critique of Asset Allocation

When it comes to retirement planning, most financial advisors miss the mark in properly diversifying portfolios. The missing ingredient is the insurance against what most U.S. investors currently own; U.S. Stocks, U.S. Corporate Bonds and U.S. Government Bonds. All of these assets are subject to U.S. dollar risk.

For decades, the typical financial advisor diversified U.S. investor portfolios as follows:

60% Stocks
30% Bonds
5% Real Estate Investment Trust (REIT), Commodities, Other
5% Cash

One's age and number of years from retirement would dictate the amount allocated to stocks. The old adage has been "subtract your age from 100 and that is the percentage you should be invested in stocks." So, if you're 55, then 100-55 = 45, thus 45% of your portfolio should be invested in stocks. But even that has been thrown out the window with the stock market run up from 2009 to record highs.

The vehicles that advisors have typically used to invest in stocks would be a mixture of U.S. Large-Cap, Mid-Cap and Small-Cap mutual funds or ETF's diversified among a wide range of sectors, with some foreign exposure. The bonds would be a mixture of mostly U.S. corporate, with some allocated to U.S. Government bonds through GNMA funds or U.S. Treasuries. The cash would be parked in U.S. money market accounts waiting for future investment opportunities.

The next graphic is a snapshot of the "diversified" allocation Charles Schwab was recommending to clients to meet their goals, based on whether their risk was conservative, moderately conservative, moderate, where most are in retirement or approaching retirement.[9]

---

[9] Charles Schwab On Investing Magazine, Summer 2009
http://www.schwab.com/public/schwab/investing/retirement_and_planning/retirement_income/portfolio_allocation

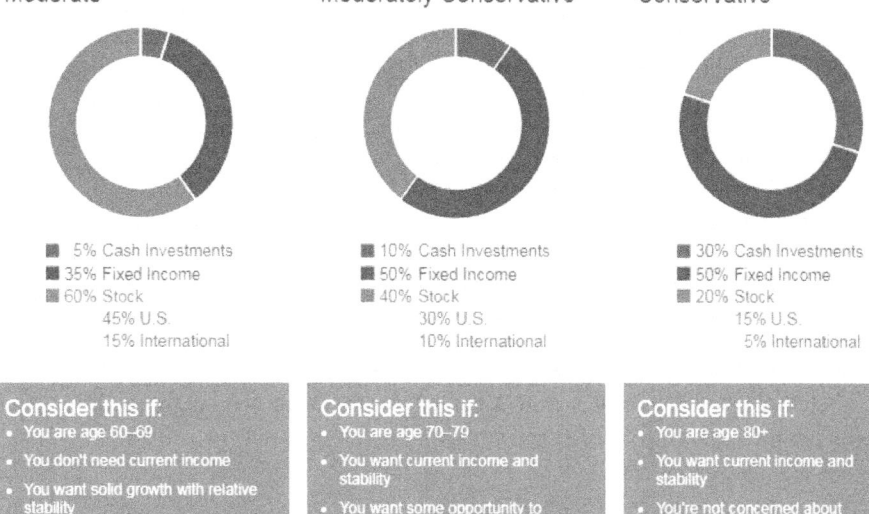

On its face, without going into sector analysis or the quality of the bonds, this seems like a well-diversified portfolio. However, there is one glaring risk that is never discussed by most advisors.

Outside of the foreign exposure in stocks, most of this diversified portfolio is subject to the risk of the U.S. dollar decline. The stocks are mostly U.S. corporations; the bonds, U.S. corporate or U.S. government and money markets are U.S. dollar-based.

Most investors don't think about currency risk. They don't realize when the U.S. dollar-based portfolio goes up 10% and the dollar falls 10%, they haven't increased the purchasing power of their wealth. They feel wealthier because all they see is that their account went up 10%, but they don't see the hidden effect of the U.S. dollar decline (inflation).

Since 2009 most every asset has done well, and gold and silver have taken a bit of a hit but maintained a base between $1200-$1350 leading up to the year 2018. Simply put, when the dollar moves up, gold moves lower and vice versa.

Bonds also have done well overall and only CD's haven't been paying out as much as they used to. The dollar moving higher has benefited all these too from 2009 to 2018. Plus, the Fed keeping rates artificially low has benefited bonds and stocks. The chart we saw earlier of the dollar falling to the low 70's though is approximately 30% lower than where we are today. Can we get there again? What protection does your portfolio have in case for some reason we do have a dollar decline?

Some advisors will claim the foreign allocation to stocks will make up for this U.S. dollar risk, but when the Dow was in the process of losing 46.8% to the low in 2008, as the dollar fell from its high of 120 to 74, almost all foreign markets got hammered as you can see from the synopsis of many foreign markets below.

- Japan (NIKKEI) Down 80.6%
- Germany (DAX) Down 47.7%
- Great Britain (FTSE) Down 41.7%
- China (SSE) Down 62.5%
- Every country's stock Index was down more than 40%, with most down more than 50% from their all-time highs.

Other advisors will counter that real estate investments like REITs will hedge against a U.S. dollar decline but higher rates typically hurt real estate investments and we are destined for higher rates once the deflationary contraction episode ends (explained further in Chapter 4).

Stock Markets at All Time Highs

Asset allocation models tell us to take from what is at the highs and put it into what is at the lows. The stock market through 2018 was hitting all-time highs over and over. It was the most overbought market ever. Gold and silver have been flirting with the $1050 to $1,400 level through 2018, much lower than the 2011 highs. Knowing where you are in a cycle is what helps you know whether you are getting a good buy on an asset. Nothing goes straight up, and nothing goes straight down. But it is true that the dollar, over time, loses its purchasing power and gold, over time, maintains its purchasing power. That's why having gold as a hedge for your U.S. dollar currency risk is a must for your portfolio and as of 2018, it's priced at a discount to the 2011 highs.

The best example we can give to explain the importance of maintaining metals in your portfolio can be found in the case of what was actual money at one point in time in the U.S. The 1964 U.S. quarter used to buy close to a gallon of gas in 1964. It contained 90% silver. Today, if you exchange that silver into the scrip of the day (dollars and cents), you'll find that that same quarter can buy you about a gallon of gas. A 1965 quarter in 1965 could buy you about a gallon of gas. Today, that same quarter, which is in existence today, can only buy you 25 cents worth of gas. And that is what the government has done to our money. Read this paragraph a second time and think over what it is really saying about government being in our best interest.

Starting today and moving forward, which would you think will hold its purchasing power? The 1964 quarter or the 1965 quarter. You really don't have to read another sentence in this book to be convinced that metals need to be a part of your portfolio, and this example is exactly why I am writing this book and updating it for this printing. Most still do not see this correlation, but soon enough will. Will this presentation I put forth in this book be enough for you to act is something only you can answer. After reading this book, you'll answer this question for yourself as I won't be using fear tactics, just pointing out real data so you can make a good decision.

Chapter 2
<u>A Brief History of Gold and Federal Reserve Notes</u>

History has shown that gold has been used as money since before the time of Jesus Christ. History has also revealed the weakness of currencies when governments abuse their powers. The Roman Empire rose to great heights when it could go from country to country and conquer it, taking the gold and paying their soldiers. But when there were no more countries to conquer and take gold from, they started debasing the gold coins paid to soldiers to keep them paid and happy. And when the soldiers complained about receiving the lighter and lighter weight coins, with the government not capable of compensating them any other way, the Empire collapsed. This is how all empires eventually end; the debasement of currency.

Our modern-day paper money experiment began with the creation of the Federal Reserve Act in 1913 and the introduction of Federal Reserve Notes, (FRNs). FRNs used to be exchanged for gold coin as we have explained and that ended in 1933 with the confiscation of gold during the Franklin D. Roosevelt era.

The reason for the confiscation was the run on banks, which saw over 10,000 banks close as people rushed to exchange their FRNs for gold. President Roosevelt put an end to this run by ordering citizens to turn in their gold to the government or face fines and imprisonment. The good citizens trusted their government and did as they were told, as it became illegal to own any gold worth than $100. In exchange for this trust, U.S. citizens were given $20 of FRNs for each ounce of gold they possessed.

Then in 1934, President Roosevelt devalued those FRNs by 60%, as his administration artificially raised the price of gold from $20 an ounce to $35 an ounce. Your $100 of cash you just got for the gold was still worth $100, but your $100 of gold you still had in your pocket was worth 75% more.

For the next 37 years, the price of gold held steady, and by August of 1971 gold averaged $42.72 an ounce. The reason for this period of stability is that FRNs and other currencies of the world were still tied to gold via fixed exchange rates. While U.S. citizens couldn't buy more than $100 of gold, the Central Banks of the world still were involved in what was known as a gold exchange standard.

From the New York Federal Reserve:

> "This system was put in place in 1944, when the leaders of Allied nations met at Bretton Woods, New Hampshire, to set up a stable economic structure out of the chaos of World War II. The U.S. dollar was fixed at $35 per ounce of gold and all other currencies were expressed in terms of dollars.
>
> The Bretton Woods system began to weaken in the 1960s, when foreigners accumulated large amounts of U.S. dollars from post-World War II aid and sales of their exports in the United States. There were concerns as to whether the U.S. had enough gold to redeem all the dollars.
>
> With reserves of gold falling steadily, the situation could not be sustained and the U.S. decided to abandon this system. In 1971, President Nixon announced that U.S. dollars would no longer be convertible into gold. By 1973, this action led to the system of floating exchange rates that exist today."[1]

Within three years of the Nixon decoupling of the U.S. dollar from gold, inflation rates hit double digits. Many were afraid their dollars would become worthless. 1973 and 1974 were bad years for the stock market seeing the Dow lose 46.3%. Gold, meanwhile, more than quadrupled in price, going from the low-$40 range to over $180 an ounce by December of 1974. There was much uncertainty during this time. Can history repeat? We'll address this later in the book.

In 1975, U.S. citizens were finally allowed to own more than $100 worth of gold through the passing of a bill signed by President Gerald Ford legalizing private ownership of gold coins, bars and certificates.

Gold was trading at $175 an ounce at the beginning of 1975. The nation was in the midst of an inflationary period which saw the

---

[1] Gold Exchange Standard; New York Federal Reserve
http://www.newyorkfed.org/education/fx/foreign.html

inflation rate hit a high of 12.34% and fall to a low of 6.34% by February of 1978.

The price of gold fell and languished for a few years as inflation subsided but broke to a new high in 1978 hitting the $180 range again; the calm before the storm.

By March of 1979, the inflation rate hit double digits again and broke out to almost 14% by January of 1980. Gold during this time went to its then all-time closing high on January 21st at $850 an ounce.

During this run-up in the price of gold, the U.S. government needed to pull a rabbit out of its Federal Reserve hat to subdue the concern citizens had about the economy, and especially the plummeting value of the U.S. dollar compared to gold. That "rabbit" was provided with the installing of Paul Volcker as Fed Chairman in August of 1979. Within a short time of leading the Fed, Volcker instituted an interest rate policy that increased the Federal Funds Rate to much higher levels.[2] He did this after consulting John Exter as witnessed by Exter's son-in-law Barry Downs who sat in on the meeting and I had the pleasure of interviewing to see what exactly went on during that meeting.

Volcker asked Exter what to do and Exter replied, "loosen monetary policy."

As interest paid on bank savings, CDs and money markets started to increase, Americans clamored to take advantage, thus dumping gold. The inflation rate came all the way down to the mid 2% range by 1983.

What was unique about this era was that there had been no wars involving the U.S. since the end of the Vietnam War in 1975. There was no real competition to the U.S. dollar at that time except for gold. Paying higher interest rates restored confidence in the almighty dollar. These higher interest rates will be coming again, and it won't be pretty for most of you and your portfolios. Gold will take off higher and the Fed will be asking the question; what do we do? Their balance sheet is

---

[2] Federal Funds Data; New York Federal Reserve
http://www.newyorkfed.org/markets/omo/dmm/fedfundsdata.cfm

already a mess today as you'll see shortly. The real answer is, they can't do much to stop what's coming.

Gold languished for 17 years after Volcker's moves, hitting a bottom of $252.80 in July of 1999.

Gold started to bounce off its low, and in mid-1999 moved higher with the "end of the world" rhetoric accompanying the looming expiration of the 20th century. While the bounce wasn't that large, gold did maintain a mid-to upper-$200 price for the next couple of years, never falling below its 1999 low.

This is where financial advisors will tell you that when you include all of these down years in the price of gold, it doesn't paint a pretty picture for overall returns if you begin your analysis from say the high price of 1980. For the most part, they are right. It was in the 80's that Ronald Reagan began the unprecedented government spending that hasn't ceased since. The "faith" in the dollar has kept the price of gold depressed overall. But something changed in 1999 that wasn't a factor before. This "something" was the introduction of the Euro.

The first year or so of a new financial instrument is sometimes a probationary period to see how it will do compared to the competition. The Euro during 1999 fell to where it was at par with the dollar by the dawn of the 21st century. By October of 2000, though, the Euro had already bottomed against the dollar.

Gold prices during this time frame of the introduction of the Euro languished. This was due in part to the September 1999 Central Bank Gold Agreement by G10 countries to dump 2000 tonnes of gold on the open market over the next five years ending in 2004.[3] So not only was the price of gold affected by the faith in the dollar and government printing more and more money, but central banks also began selling some of their hoard.

However, even with the dumping of gold on the open market, gold managed to break $300 an ounce in 2003 and $400 per ounce by 2004 in anticipation of the end to the Central Bank selling of gold.

---

[3] World Gold Council; The Central Bank Gold Agreement, September 26, 1999
http://www.reserveasset.gold.org/central_bank_agreements/cbga1/

The Euro Joined Gold as Competition to the U.S. Dollar

The Euro had bounced off its lows and had become a much stronger currency. As the dollar was sinking from its high in 2002, and the uncertainty of what effect central bank sales would have on the price of gold, the Euro became the only other safe haven in the minds of those looking to get out of the dollar.

The central banks were still busy making sure the price of gold wouldn't take off. They see gold as competition to their fiat scheme. As the first Central Bank Sales Agreement ended, a second Agreement took its place in March of 2004, to last five more years. This time the agreement was to sell 2,500 tonnes of gold.[4]

I wonder how much the Swiss citizens enjoyed their central bank selling gold, as all the while the price was moving higher. What would U.S. citizens do if the U.S. started to dump its gold on the market? The truth is, we don't even know what gold the government really has since the government never allows it to be audited. It's *supposed* to be around 8,033 tonnes, as that is what they have on the books.[5] We just have to trust them that it is there and has not been lent out. If it is there it gives the confidence (illusion?) that your money is somehow backed by gold, when in reality most in government and the Federal Reserve would prefer not to possess any gold. One must wonder why most central banks of the world own gold. It indeed is an illusion that it is backing your pieces of paper that make up your countries currency. I mean seriously, gold produces nothing, just sits there and pays no interest. Yet somehow over time, the world over, it maintains its purchasing power in every currency. Yet throughout history, 609 currencies have already failed. Why? Because of government overreach.[6]

---

[4] World Gold Council; The Central Bank Gold Agreement 2, March 8, 2004
http://www.reserveasset.gold.org/central_bank_agreements/cbga2/
[5] Is There Any Gold In Ft. Knox? Lew Rockwell interview with Ron Paul
http://www.lewrockwell.com/lewrockwell-show/2010/05/09/149-is-there-any-gold-in-ft-knox/
[6] http://www.rapidtrends.com/history-of-fiat-and-paper-money-failures/

The Competition to the Dollar Has Grown

During the time frame of 1971-1999, there really wasn't any competition to the U.S. dollar. The U.S. dollar was king of the world. The U.S. education system simply did not deem gold a worthy subject, except for tales of a couple of discoveries; the California Gold Rush of the 1850s and an Alaskan Klondike gold unearthing of the 1890s.

What helped gold move higher after 2000 was the ability to invest in it more easily with the introduction of Exchange Traded Funds like GLD in 2004. Fund managers now had an easy way to diversify into the metal.

The price of gold went up every year in U.S. dollar terms from 2000 to 2012. This entire rise in gold has occurred despite Central Bank Sales Agreements to suppress the price of gold.

Year End	Price of Gold
2000	$ 273.60
2001	$ 279.00
2002	$ 348.20
2003	$ 416.10
2004	$ 438.40
2005	$ 518.90
2006	$ 638.00
2007	$ 838.00
2008	$ 885.50
2009	$1,087.50
2010	$1,405.50
2011	$1,531.00
2012	$1,657.50
2013	$1,204.50
2014	$1,206
2015	$1,060
2016	$1,145.90
2017	$1,291.00
2018+	Much Higher

All governments of the world are dealing with the same problem of becoming too large for their own existence. We've already seen the effects of this growth of government in Greece and are beginning to see it in various cities throughout the United States. Even state budgets like that of Illinois are strained along with pension outlays. Heck, Illinois even has trouble paying off lottery winners because of budget issues.[7]

In fact, in all major countries today, currencies have lost ground to gold in the past 10 years, as seen in the following table.

And this is one of the most important charts you'll see because while we price currencies in each other, and that is part of the illusion I described earlier, this graph shows how gold over time outshines them all.

---

[7]http://www.chicagotribune.com/news/local/breaking/ct-lottery-delayed-payments-met-20170627-story.html

10-Year Spot Gold vs. Major Currencies[8]

The potential growth once gold gets going again is tremendous! The first chart showed in U.S. dollar terms, gold was up 326.56% in 10 years. The last 10 years it is up only 50.38%. It shows you that over the next 10 years, gold should begin to move up towards that 300% plus return. It can be higher or lower than 300%, but it's going higher nonetheless. If you are in another country outside the U.S., look to get triple digit returns in gold in the coming years as well.

---

[8] Data taken from KITCO, Gold price as of May 2010 and 2018

U.S. Dollar	326.56%
Swiss Franc	176.31%
Canadian Dollar	194.61%
Euro	199.03%
Japanese Yen	267.39%
British Pound	322.72%

The term "buy the dip" is where we are in 2018 and beyond on any downturns you may see. View any downturns as a gift. The price of gold will at some point soar to over $5,000 I think and whether it goes higher will depend on if government ever learns how to stop spending or pass laws that state they must. But I'm afraid they will fight to the end with what they perceive has worked in the past; more printing. This won't end well except for the investor in gold.

While investors watch the price of gold move up on a consistent basis in the years to come, most won't realize how much currencies lose in value compared to gold. They won't find the previous charts anywhere on CNBC.

"With the exception only of the period of the gold standard, practically all governments of history have used their exclusive power to issue money to defraud and plunder the people."
—Nobel Prize winner F.A. von Hayek

Chapter 3
Flaws of the Financial Services Industry

A critique of the Pyramid of Financial Risk, Modern Portfolio Theory and the Prudent Man Rule or "What Financial Advisors Pass Off as Advice for Diversification.

The Investment Pyramid

Gold was the money of our forefathers. Today, if they were alive, they'd demand their portraits be removed from U.S. currency. They would be upset that the currency today has seen the U.S. government abuse their powers since 1913 and taken away its relationship to sound money; gold, and later silver.

Financial advisors aren't taught anything about gold as a viable investment, let alone as insurance for one's U.S. dollar exposure. Gold sits atop the pyramid of risk they developed as being "high risk," while the U.S. dollar sits at the bottom, representing "low risk." How can an asset that once was money be categorized today as high risk?

You'll recall from the introduction that you could bury gold in your back yard 10 years ago, dig it up today, and see that it never changed. It's the same gold and has close to the same purchasing power. But bury FRN's in your back yard 10 years ago and dig them up today, and you'll find you can't purchase as much with that money. Which one of these has more risk if you based your answer on purchasing power over time?

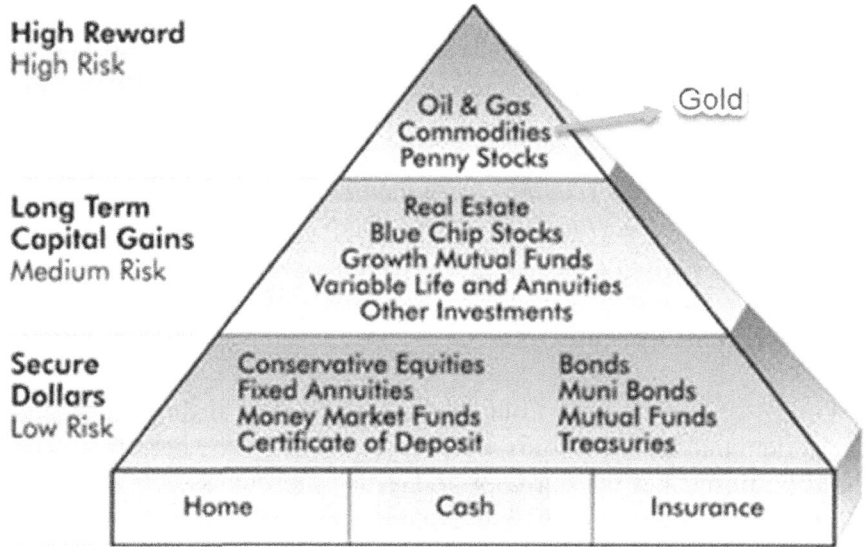

The Investment Pyramid Flaw

Financial advisors aren't taught anything about gold as a viable asset to allocate your funds to because their perception has been that gold is a risky investment as seen in the Investment Pyramid (above). This investment pyramid is one of the first things you learn about asset allocation when you become a financial advisor. At one point in time, I was one and know from always asking questions since that time what advisors know about gold. Most know nothing and don't' recommend it to investors.

The big financial firms on Wall Street would have you believe mutual funds, municipal bonds and equities are a better risk as you see them just above cash. Naturally most investors do this and invest accordingly. In all honesty, they have been good investments over time. I do not deny that, and pretend gold should be one's only investment. But as you'll see when we speak about asset allocation, there is a time for cash, stocks, bonds and commodities. Each has their day. With a properly diversified portfolio, investments in all of these assets reduce overall risk. This is especially true when the stock market is hitting new all-time high after all-time high. Whatever point in time you are reading this book, you'll see at some point a stock market decline (how severe we don't know) and a rise in the price of gold (how much we do not know).

Financial advisors have been trained by the industry to lean heavily towards stocks. There are only a select few who give any credit to gold as part of a diversified portfolio.

Even the financial advisors who obtain further education and obtain their Certified Financial Planner (CFP) credential from the College for Financial Planning are somewhat misinformed on gold. The CFP designation sets advisors apart, as they will have taken the extra steps to educate themselves further and be of better service to their clients. All in all, I think this is great and recommend these advisors over others.

I was planning on becoming a CFP back in 2002 when I was working as a financial advisor. I wanted to be the best possible advisor for my clients and this designation is what was needed at the time according to industry experts. When I paid for my six courses and purchased all the books required for each section, I briefly went through the book supplied for the investment section of the course. The book was *Investments: An Introduction,* Seventh Edition, by Herbert B. Mayo (Custom Edition: College for Financial Planning)[1].

This book had six pages devoted to gold, almost all of them negative about gold being a good investment. It referred to gold as "jewelry" and "numismatic coins," and didn't even mention American Gold Eagle bullion coins made here in the United States by the U.S. Mint. Instead, it mentioned the Canadian Maple Leaf gold coin, which the author described as being "of particular interest to gold collectors." This is simply a laughable synopsis of the gold market and showed the author was clueless and just grabbed a few bits of info and passed it off to the reader as expertise on precious metals. It was then I lost respect for the financial services industry in general and decided to

---

[1] *Investments: An Introduction* by Herbert B. Mayo
https://www.amazon.com/Investments-Introduction-Herbert-B-Mayo/dp/1133936520

become an expert in precious metals. That took me 8 more years of getting to know the industry and even working for a gold dealer to discover their inside secrets which I'll get to in Chapter 8.

There was no mention of bullion bars and coins in that CFP investment book as means to hedge U.S. dollar risk. There was not one statement about silver in the entire book, yet silver was our money until 1964.

In the introduction, I mentioned that gold is just a shiny metal. It is what gold is *priced in* that changes. If investors see that gold has appreciated more than 50% versus the dollar the last 10 years, they'll realize it is the *dollar* that has the "higher risk" and gold the "lower risk." And remember, these last 10 years included a big downturn in the price of gold. What asset do you as an investor own to protect their portfolio from this dollar risk? Unfortunately for most, the answer is probably not much.

On a side note they put one's home as a low risk with cash in the investment pyramid. Do they realize that a home depreciates over time because of wear and tear and that the real estate market offers a good time to buy and a good time to sell too? 2018 may have well been another top in the real estate market, especially with higher end property and the elimination of the ability to write off interest on the loan.

However, the problem with the financial services industry doesn't stop there. The problems can also be traced back to the Prudent Man Rule, developed in the late 1950's.

The Prudent Man Rule

The Prudent Man Rule was created in 1959 and updated in 1992 as the Restatement of Trusts 2d: Prudent Man Rule:

> Uniform Prudent Investor Act Section 1. Prudent Investor Rule. (a) Except as otherwise provided in subsection (b), a trustee who invests and manages trust assets owes a duty to the beneficiaries of the trust to comply with the prudent investor rule set forth in this [Act].[2]

Under this rule, "the trustee is under a duty to the beneficiary to use reasonable care and skill to preserve the trust property and make it productive."

One might expect this requirement of care from any financial advisor managing the portfolios of investors today. However, the kinds of investments inferred by the Act might need to be updated.

The Prudent Man Rule Flaw

From the Act:

Ordinarily it is proper for a trustee to invest in government securities, such as bonds of the United States or of the State or of municipalities, in first mortgages on land, or in corporate bonds.

There has been risk associated with each one of these "proper" investments. The major risk is with U.S. dollar depreciation, but even municipal bonds are at risk, as this NY Times article excerpt shows:

The biggest risk is with long bond. Interest rates are unpredictable. They go up 100 basis points or 1 percentage point and you could lose 20 to 30 percent of your investment.[3]

What was the prudent investor doing in the early 1930s when there was a run on the banks? They were exchanging their FRNs for gold. Investors listen to financial advisors and couldn't tell you one iota about the dollar risk they're taking. They do however know how to

---

[2] Trust Examination Manual - Appendix C – Fiduciary Law - Uniform Prudent Investor Act -Prudent Investor Rule
http://www.fdic.gov/regulations/examinations/trustmanual/appendix_c/appendix_c.html#_toc497113666
[3] TMunicipal Bond Defaults Shake Up a Once-Sedate Market
https://www.nytimes.com/2016/04/23/your-money/municipal-bond-defaults-shake-up-a-once-sedate-market.html?_r=0

calculate commissions or how to take their cut off the top when managing your money when an Index Fund can do the same thing.

Today we have the Federal Reserve, SEC, NASD and many, many more regulating bodies to "protect" us from unscrupulous investments, yet they couldn't see the problems leading up to the financial crisis of 2009...... nor did most financial advisors who were acting prudently. Today is no different from 2009, except now there's trillions more debt to deal with. Eventually this will weigh heavily on the U.S. dollar when inflation settles in and interest rates shoot higher and gold will be the safety net for many.

Modern Portfolio Theory

I'm going to get a little more technical now with you but bear with me. I have been told my writing style is such that I can explain things that are complicated, so most can comprehend and the last thing I want to do is have you not understand anything I am saying. This might be a good point for that cup of coffee.

It was just before the American Law Institutes' approval of the Prudent Man Rule that Harry Markowitz was receiving his Nobel Prize (1990 Economics) for his lecture on Modern Portfolio Theory (MPT).

In a nutshell, MPT attempts to create an optimal portfolio by identifying a client's risk tolerance. To do so would take care of the two kinds of risk that are prevalent (according to MPT); Systematic Risk (like recessions and wars) that cannot be diversified away, and Unsystematic Risk that can be diversified away with more share ownership.

Investing with the appropriate amount of diversification and risk tolerance will lead the investor to an "efficient" portfolio. To optimize this efficient portfolio, the Sharpe Ratio is analyzed, which reveals the amount of additional return above the "risk-free" rate a portfolio provides compared to the risk it carries. The further you go away from risk free, the better the potential return, but additional risk materializes.[4]

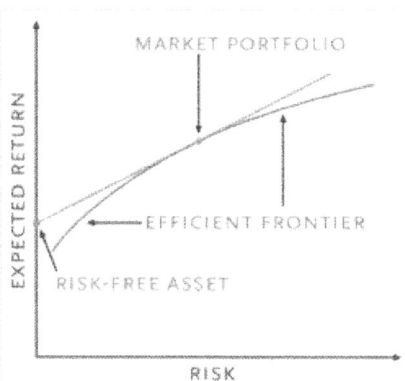

A "risk-free" asset in this case, according to MPT, could be the 91-day Treasury Note, 10-year Treasury Bonds, or other government-backed securities.

The Modern Portfolio Theory Flaw

It's easy to be a Monday morning quarterback and critique investment theory after the fact. Criticism could have been levied against MPT in 2008 and 2009, as there wasn't an "efficient frontier" for investors, leaving them and their advisors scratching their heads as to what to do next. This is not the flaw of MPT I wish to address.

The flaw I'm addressing is the assumption that there is such a thing as a "risk-free" asset.

The assumption is claiming the U.S. dollar or government treasuries are risk-free.

Yes, the dollar had a good track record up until about the year 2000. This was addressed earlier, as there was no competition to the U.S. dollar. But as the 21st century arrived, there surfaced more places investors could park money, including the Euro and subsequently gold via the many Exchange Traded Funds (ETFs).

---

[4] Sharpe Ratio http://www.investopedia.com/terms/s/sharperatio.asp

But there are times when U.S. treasuries lose money. That time is when interest rates rise. The Federal Reserve through open market operations however has kept interest rates historically low since the times of Reagan. The Federal Reserve has treasuries on their own balance sheet. Economist John Exter is on the record when this figure first hit $400 billion that he was concerned about the Fed's balance sheet. Today that number is over $4.4 trillion, which is $3.4 trillion more than before the crisis. The Fed finally started addressing its balance sheet and said they would start liquidating some of it, to the tune of around $10 billion a month. At that rate it would take the Fed 27 years to reduce their balance sheet back to what it was however they did promise to ratchet that up to $50 billion a month in short time. Promises, promises. In 2018 interest rates were already starting to climb at the beginning of the year. Personally, I see them plateau again and then decrease and more Fed quantitative easing enters the picture, but we will get into that in Chapter 4.

The concerns with the balance sheets of the U.S. and Federal Reserve clearly show there is risk as to whether this game they are playing with our economy can keep us from a recession. The adding of debt to debt does not bode well for the future. We've seen the National Debt move over $20 trillion and the Fed's balance sheet over $4.4 trillion and interest rates have stayed artificially low with treasuries stable. What could go wrong? You the investor need to know the risk of what higher interest rates will bring to these "risk free" assets from the government.

What was once viewed as "risk-free" in the days of the creation of MPT, when we were in our "heyday," is now viewed by astute investors as an asset that bears quite a bit of risk.

Gold Counteracts the Decline of the U.S. Dollar

For the most part, only gold can counteract the fall of the U.S. dollar. Silver has done well too, which we'll see in Part II.

There are other avenues to counteract inflation, like Treasury Inflation Protected Securities (TIPS) and I have nothing against putting some money in them as part of a diversified portfolio.[5]

However, TIPS are no substitute for gold, as some advisors would have you believe.[6] They are a hedge against the government-manipulated CPI figures which have conveniently left out energy and real estate. Ask any senior receiving social security how their payments keep up with the prices of things they have been buying each year with the additional cost of living adjustment they receive based on the CPI. The government likes it when they don't have to pay out increases and calculate inflation conveniently low, so they keep manipulating the CPI in their favor to pay out less to social security recipients.

Recognizing Flaws

It doesn't take a Nobel Prize to spot a flaw in the system and see the failures to counteract the fall of the dollar. Congress dictates policy and regulates the economy with citizens' best interest in mind, right? But since when has a budget come out as planned? It's only a matter of time before these flaws reveal themselves. Your portfolio needs to account for the potential for dollar weakness and add some insurance against it with gold and silver which we'll provide even more reasoning to do so throughout this book.

---

[5] Treasury Direct - Treasury Inflation-Protected Securities (TIPS)
http://www.treasurydirect.gov/indiv/products/prod_tips_glance.htm
[6] Social Security's new math: Who loses? reported by Lisa Scherzer for SmartMoney
http://articles.moneycentral.msn.com/RetirementandWills/RetireInStyle/social-securitys-new-math-who-loses.aspx

Chapter 4
How A Deflationary Credit Contraction Unfolds

Economic Cycles – If our economists, financial advisors, Congress and the Federal Reserve missed the 2008-2009 crisis, what gives anyone confidence they'll see the next one coming? Doug Eberhardt

Opening Thoughts Pertaining to This Chapter

Government and Federal Reserve intervention in economic cycles has the propensity of creating crisis, not preventing it. The absurd choices of our elected representatives stem from their inability to live within the country's taxable means fueled by a Federal Reserve that is reactive, not proactive to market signals. In other words, they can't see what's coming. This chapter will lay the groundwork to what I see coming, not with speculation, but with a hard look at the root problems our country faces in the future.

In writing this chapter, I had to pull observations from multiple sources and put them together, so the reader can visualize just what's going on. The good news is I don't have to throw out formulas and what not like some Keynesian economist who also didn't see the last crisis coming. But in putting these pieces together from an economic perspective, it was like taking a 1,000-piece puzzle of a portrait of a perfectly blue sky and trying to figure out which piece goes where when all the pieces look the same. Most people when it comes to economics conclude; "it's all Greek to me." And even among economists you'll hear opposing views.

Piece by piece, I have put together the data based on the works of Austrian economists and financial experts who utilize Austrian economic theory along with my own conclusions that I think improve upon those theories. Yes, even the Austrians disagree with each other and take sides on who historically they follow.

Collectively, after reading this detailed chapter, one will be able to visualize just what kind of economic and financial mess our leaders have levied upon us and our heirs and yes, their heirs also. By the time you finish this chapter and have a better understanding of where we are, you'll be able to decipher for yourself whether gold makes sense for your portfolio. My Illusions of Wealth book takes this chapter and expands upon it in detail as well as analyzing our monetary, economic and banking and Federal Reserve system and taking a look at other investment strategies. But what you get here is the synopsis of important issues you need to consider before investing in precious metals.

Naturally, many may already be convinced that they need to be in gold and silver after reading the first few chapters based on maintaining purchasing power and looking at what really backs the U.S. dollar. This chapter takes the conversation to a new level, as it is important to expose the depth of the problem with our credit-and debt-based economy. Before you get into what gold and silver to buy, it's important, if you are going to be able to convince others to read and understand this material for their own benefit, that you can give them some fundamental understanding as to why the U.S. economy is based on a house of sand (debt) and how it can turn on a dime the opposite direction. In fact, we already saw our monetary system turn on a dime when the government deems it necessary as we pointed out when in 1964 they changed the dime from 90% silver to a dime that under 2 cents in actual melt value with the metal it's made from.

Definitions

The first issue that needs to be resolved before diving into any analysis is determining the proper definitions of the various terms used throughout the chapter. Before getting into the actual analysis, please review the Glossary at the end of this book first. It will help you understand some of the jargon used.

The last thing the mainstream economists and media want is for their hand to be exposed, so they ridicule all they can those who speak the truth. They expect that if you hear their version of a story based on their definitions, over and over enough times, then it must be true. This chapter will give you the ability to decipher their version and separate fact from fiction for yourself, so you can articulate reality to friends and family and not look like you're the crazy one at the dinner table.

The economists today aren't calling for any potential issues that are forthcoming and everyone goes about their investing with no worries once again. This chapter will hopefully wake a few people up. But in early 2017, all the talk has been about how great the future is going to be with a Trump Presidency as the DOW broke 20,000 for the first time and moved past 26,000 in the beginning of 2018.

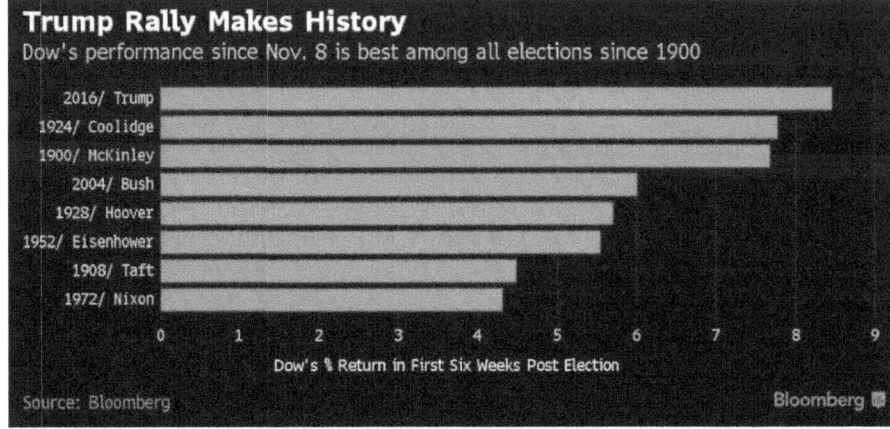

But are we close to a top in the stock market? Can one still invest in stocks and bonds and expect a continued run higher? How close are you to retirement and what risks do you want to take at this point? I'm here to tell you that there are issues in the economy to consider, not just in the U.S. but globally.

And the light shineth in darkness; and the darkness comprehended it not.

—John 1:5

I provide a synopsis of what has already occurred in the U.S. in the next two sections as it sets up what is to come.

Credit Expansion and Inflation

During an inflationary credit expansion, the supply of money is increased through the process of fractional reserve banking on the one hand and credit on the other through loans from Fed to the U.S. government.

Fractional reserve banking is the process whereby a bank will take a customer's deposit, retain a portion as reserves, and loan out the remaining portion multiple times. It is a way to create money out of thin air without using the printing press and it is an area that pretty much no one understands. Where else but a bank can you take a deposit of money and loan not just that client's money (yours) out to others, but do it over and over up to 9 times while only maintaining on hand 10% of the deposit?

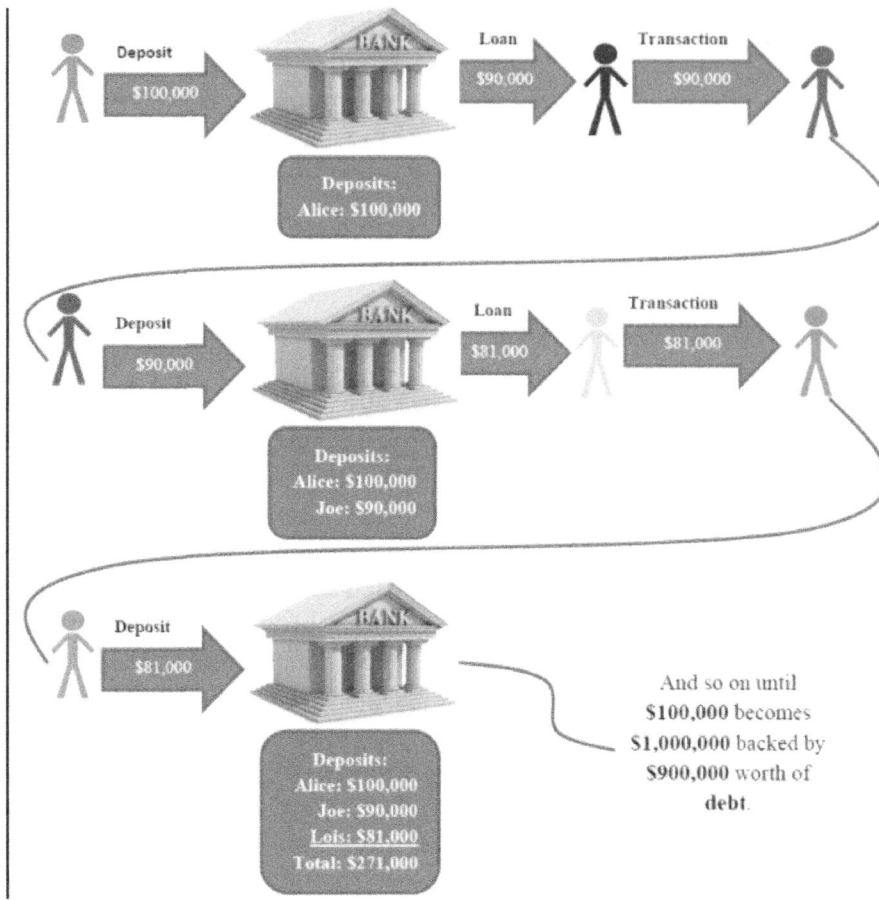

What happens when the original depositor wants his money back?

Say you deposit $100,000 in a bank and the bank does all the above while maintaining $10,000 (10%). A few months later you want to take out the $100,000 and some small interest maybe and the bank has already loaned it out several times. They have to find a way to get you the $100,000 and through the pressing of a few buttons and some help from the Federal Reserve, you're made whole. Of course, if you tried to take it out in cash you might have to wait a few days after being questioned over and over again why you want it in cash.

But what happens when a few of these people or businesses the bank loaned money to default on the loan? This is what happens when an economy sours and what happened leading up to the last crisis with subprime lending. It becomes a vicious cycle as money deflates when depositors withdraw funds and consumers default on their loans because they lose jobs or can't afford to pay mortgages any longer.

Every business cycle has the characteristics of an inflationary boom followed by, as Murray Rothbard, puts it, "a subsequent credit contraction touching off liquidation of credit and investments, bankruptcies, and deflationary price declines."[1]

The same cycle occurred during the Great Depression, when in 1932, interest rates were lowered through government manipulation and the Hoover administration pursued inflationary policies, an eerie similarity to the policies practiced by the Federal Reserve who had been trying forever to get to 2% inflation through 2018 and failing.

It was in the 30's, according to Rothbard in the book *America's Great Depression*, foreigners lost confidence in the dollar, Americans lost confidence in banks and inflation by the government turned into deflation by the policies of the public and the banks.[2] We have Japan, China and our U.S. citizens who own treasuries relying on a U.S. government to continue juggling the interest rates in a search for growth when growth has been subdued and credit has grown as you'll see shortly.

It is the credit expansion through this fractional reserve banking and Federal Reserve loans to Congress to pay for their spending plans that creates the potential for massive deflation to the point of "wiping out the greater part of the money supply," according to Pepperdine University Professor George Reisman. He says we "have seen that the process of credit expansion is capable of creating checking deposits more than 100 times as large as the reserves that support them."[3]

When the economy is expanding, the government continues spending and this is supposed to help stimulate the economy even more according to Keynesian economists. We have already discussed

---

[1] P. 103 *The Mystery of Banking* Murray Rothbard 1983
[2] P. 303-306 *America's Great Depression* Murray N. Rothbard 1963
[3] A Pro-Free-Market Program for Economic Recovery Mises Daily: November 20, 2009 by George Reisman http://mises.org/daily/3870

President Bush's $4 trillion increase and President Obama's $9 trillion addition to the National Debt. The Republican controlled House and Senate under a Trump administration passed a budget that increases the national debt by $1.5 trillion more. The inflationary policies are in full force no matter who is in the White House.

The business cycle is something many CEOs don't understand, let alone the average individual. But the Austrian School of Economic Thought comes closer than anyone else in describing what's going to happen when governments overextend. As economist Murray Rothbard reveals, "Only the Austrian theory holds the inflationary boom to be wholly unfortunate and sees the full depression as necessary to eliminate distortions introduced by the boom."[4]

Bubble Always Bursts, Recession Ensues, Government Still Spends

We must understand history to decipher if we see parallels presently and thus take advantage of those types of investments that can appreciate. In the beginning of the first chapter I discussed the government definitions of what really backs the dollar, being GDP and the labor of the people. What the Federal Reserve did by artificially lowering interest rates to try and stimulate the economy under Alan Greenspan's tenure was inflate the prices of real estate to bubble levels. This resulted in people feeling wealthier due to the newfound equity that was building up in their homes. As real estate prices rose, that wealth was put to use in buying things and supporting an expanding economy.

Equity was tapped by homeowners to pay down credit card debt, buy luxury cars, boats, take vacations and live the high life.

"Real GDP though declined from 2004 to 2007," as you can see in the following chart. It's a fact I alluded to in February of 2008 in an article cautioning investors about the economy and stock market which both crashed soon thereafter. [5,6]

---

[4] P. 75, 76 *America's Great Depression* Murray N. Rothbard 1963
[5] Bureau of Economic Analysis, U.S. Department of Commerce

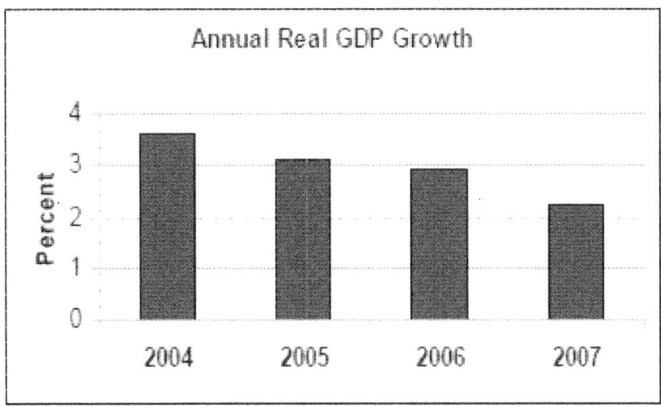

The Dow closed at 12,582.18 the day I wrote that article, yet the day before, CNBC journalist Melissa Lee was on NBC's *Today* show telling everyone to be 75% invested in stocks and "stock as much money as you can away" in them.[7] One year later the Dow was 44% lower, reaching bottom at 6,594.44 on March 5th, 2009.

GDP today isn't close to being where it has been recorded historically to consider this a strong economy. GDP has been under 4% almost the entire Obama administration, and lower than at any time in the last 70 years and has continued to stay under 4% during the Trump administration into 2018. January 2018's GDP was under 3% at 2.6%.

---

http://www.bea.gov/newsreleases/national/gdp/2008/pdf/gdp407a_fax.pdf
[6] Which Would You Prefer, Higher Taxes or Higher Inflation? By Doug Eberhardt 2/28/2008
http://buygoldandsilversafely.com/blog/budget-deficit/which-would-you-prefer-higher-taxes-or-higher-inflation/
[7] Start your midlife money checkup, Melissa Lee interview, MSNBC, 2/27/2008
http://www.msnbc.msn.com/id/21134540/vp/23368838#23368838

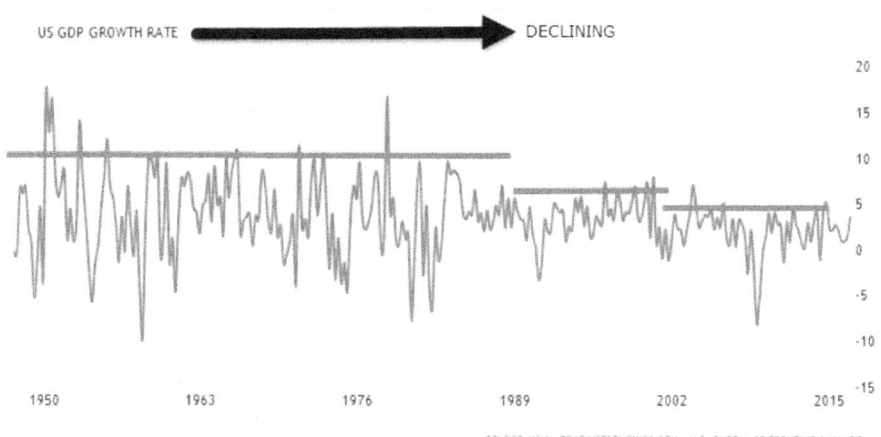

One has to ask what's driving the economy these days. We had a little blip up in GDP to a little over 3% in 2017 but since the end of the 80's, there hasn't been much growth. There are success stories such as Facebook, Apple, Netflix and Google (FANG stocks) but these companies are few and far between compared to the successes of years ago when we had companies produce things in the U.S.[8] What do Google and Facebook produce? They take from businesses in the way of advertising fees.

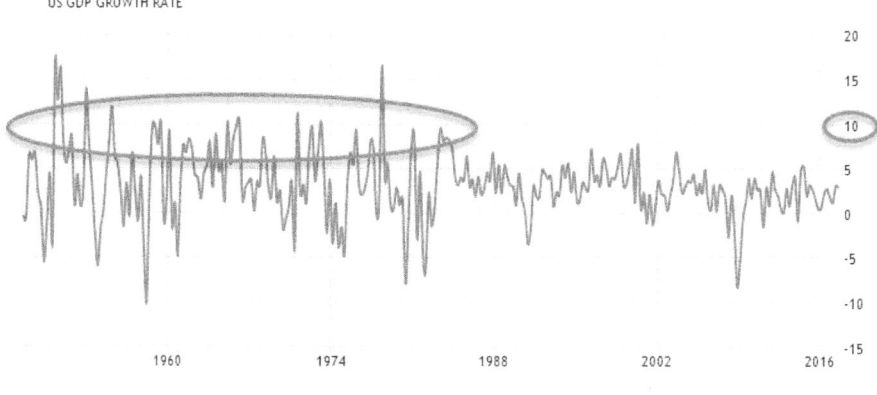

---

[8] The Economist, June 24, 2010
http://www.economist.com/node/16397124?story_id=16397124&fsrc=rss

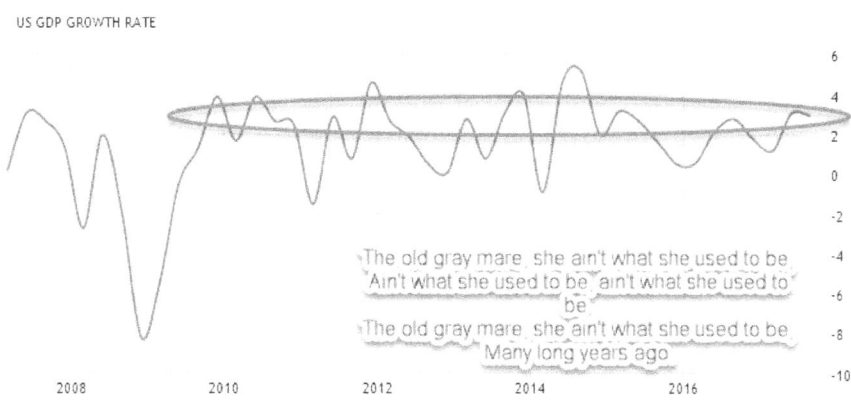

The same cycle our economy is in today is eerily like the deflationary episode that preceded the Great Depression as well as the 2008/2009 recession as January's GDP was 2.6% as I said, and December's was even revised lower. You can visualize this in the following three charts where we are show in the USA to still have not recovered.[9][10]

Notice the next graph showed the "Roaring 20s" unwinding and leading to the Great Depression. The graph after that shows the 2008/2009 recession and the third is where we are today, a prelude to what you'll see discussed further with the introduction of Exter's Pyramid and the discussion surrounding the coming deflationary credit contraction.

---

[9] The Great Recession versus the Great Depression Aiginger, http://www.economics-ejournal.org/economics/discussionpapers/2010-9/file
[10] https://www.advisorperspectives.com/dshort/updates/2017/01/27/q4-gdp-advance-estimate-real-gdp-at-1-9-worse-than-forecast

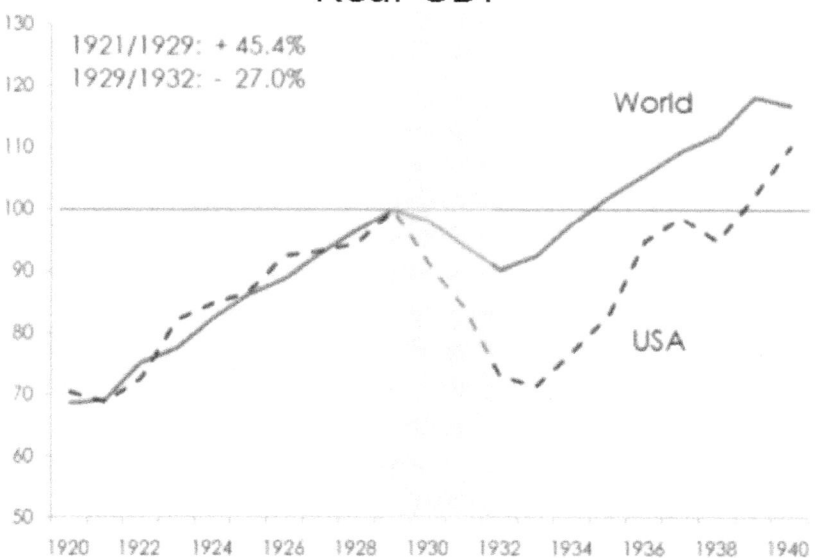

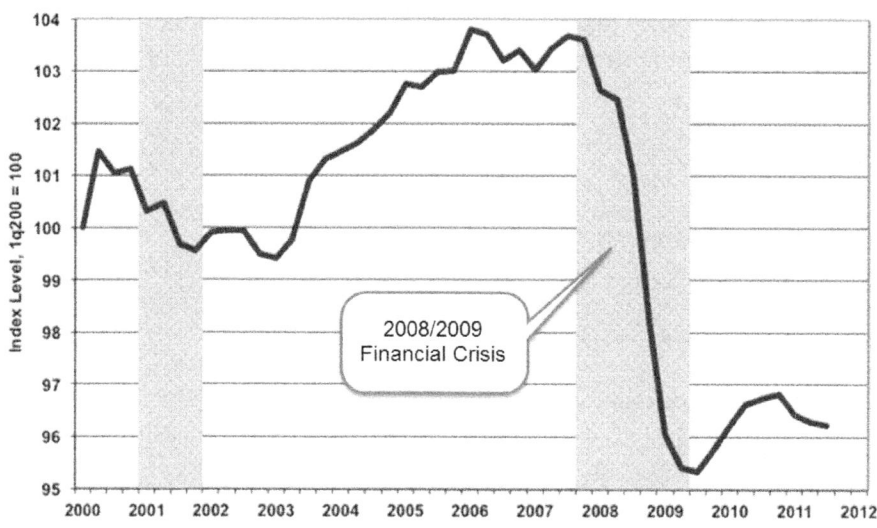

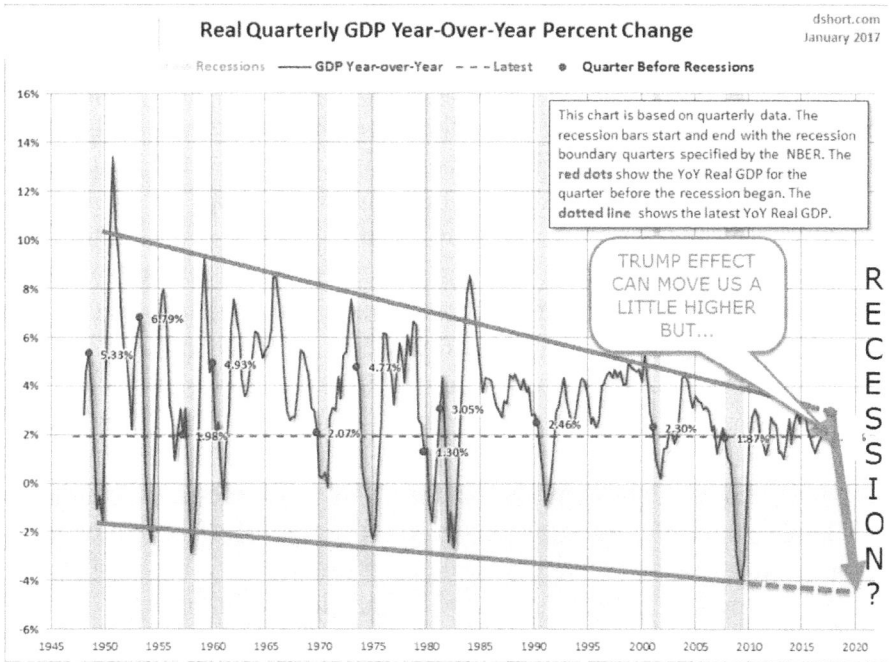

The one issue with the Trump effect on the markets though is the consumer must participate. Throwing money at infrastructure might generate some business activity and create a few jobs but doesn't produce ongoing GDP growth.

From our earlier discussion on what backs the dollar you'll recall that consumer spending is about 70% of GDP. When the consumer stops spending is when you see real GDP decline and the only thing to prop up the system is government spending.

We saw consumer spending get out of hand in 2006-2009 when equity was taken from the wealth created from people's homes and those who could see the top was forming, got out at the right time. Post crisis there was $9 trillion thrown at the economy and multiple bouts of quantitative easing which we'll discuss shortly. There were also individuals who lived beyond their means, so yes, there is a degree of self-responsibility involved. There's something to be said about awareness of where we are in the cycle of an investment (this is common sense, but most don't stop and think that buy low and sell high really does work).

However, many only heard good things out of the government and the Federal Reserve leading up to the last crisis. George W. Bush said, "we're not in a recession" in the beginning of 2008. And before that Federal Reserve chairman Alan Greenspan didn't see the bubble in housing till it popped. Former Fed Chairman Ben Bernanke didn't see the housing bubble as he took out an adjustable rate mortgage at exactly the wrong time. Fed Chairman Janet Yellen called for Fed rate hikes when the economy wasn't ready for them as inflation wasn't hitting the 2% Fed targets and found this to be a mystery yet raised rates anyway over and over. President Trump has tweeted continually about the booming stock market through 2017 into 2018. The ones who believed in the government and the Fed suffer the most and didn't see the potential of a reversal. In the end, even with a financial crisis, it is almost always the consumer who suffers, not banks, big business or the government. The latter three will find that we consumers can be smart about our investments though, as we don't have to suffer with the awareness that comes with comprehending what's really going on in the economy. We can do what we want with our investments and act accordingly.

Consumer bankruptcies were climbing even before the height of the 2009 financial crisis and in 2005 the bankruptcy laws changed. Yet even with the change in the law that was supposed to make bankruptcy more difficult and protect creditors, they rose from 2006-2009… as seen in the following chart.

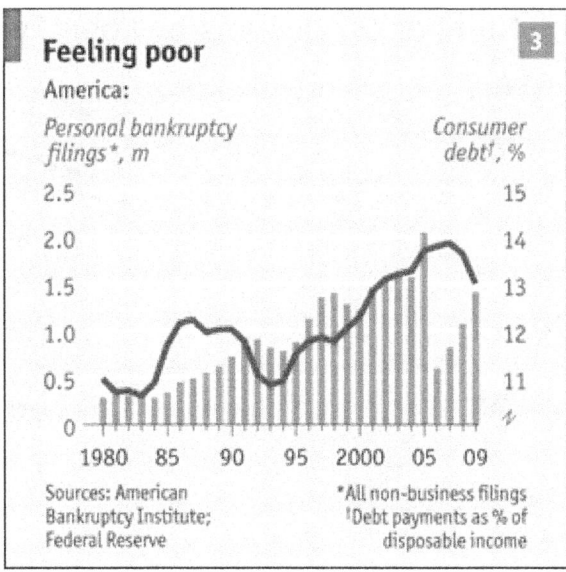

Fast forward to 2017/2018 and consumers are back at it again with their credit card debt, hitting the same high as we had right before the last crash and student and auto loans adding even more to the debt load of consumers. [11,12]

---

[11] https://www.newyorkfed.org/medialibrary/interactives/householdcredit/data/pdf/HHDC_2016Q3.pdf

[12] https://wallethub.com/edu/credit-card-debt-study/24400/

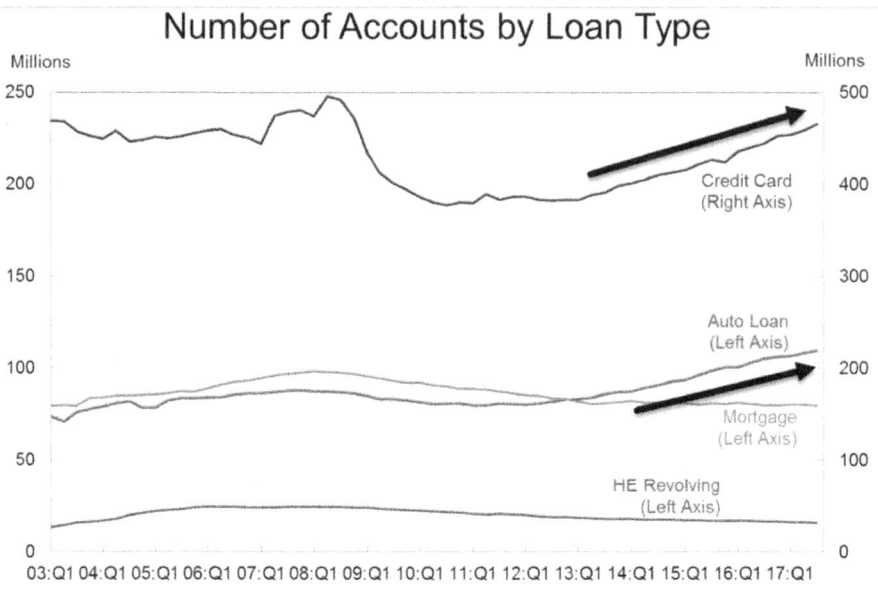

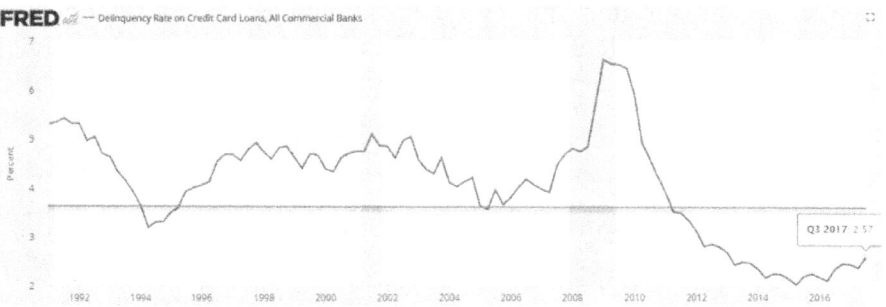

The table above shows credit card delinquency rates on the rise again beginning in the 3rd quarter of 2015 and rising every month since. When that number presently at 2.57% gets to 3.75% and above, watch out for the next recession.

According to the FDIC quarterly banking profile, failed consumer loans also dinged banks' balance sheets. Banks charged off $11.5 billion of loans in total in the first quarter, an increase of 13.4%. Net credit card charge-offs rose 22.1%, while auto loan charge-offs increased nearly 28%. Charge-offs of "other loans to individuals" increased a whopping 66.4%.[13]

Consumers never learn. Most of them it seems, unfortunately.

What could be next is exactly what you saw beginning in the 2nd quarter of 2005 all the way through the second quarter of 2009 as delinquencies increased. By the way, a good run higher in the price of gold occurred during this period. Much of the debt increase this time around has to do with subprime auto loans but also the size of student loans as college tuition costs have gotten way out of hand. Yes, we can blame the government for this too as they guarantee the loans that the colleges charge their students. There is no free market here when government backs the loans so colleges charge what they think they can and the college administrations benefit. From 1987 to 2012, universities and colleges added 517,636 administrators and professional employees, an average of 87 every working day. Now you know where the college tuition increases go. Thank your government! They'll make slaves of us all yet!

---

[13] https://www.fdic.gov/bank/analytical/qbp/

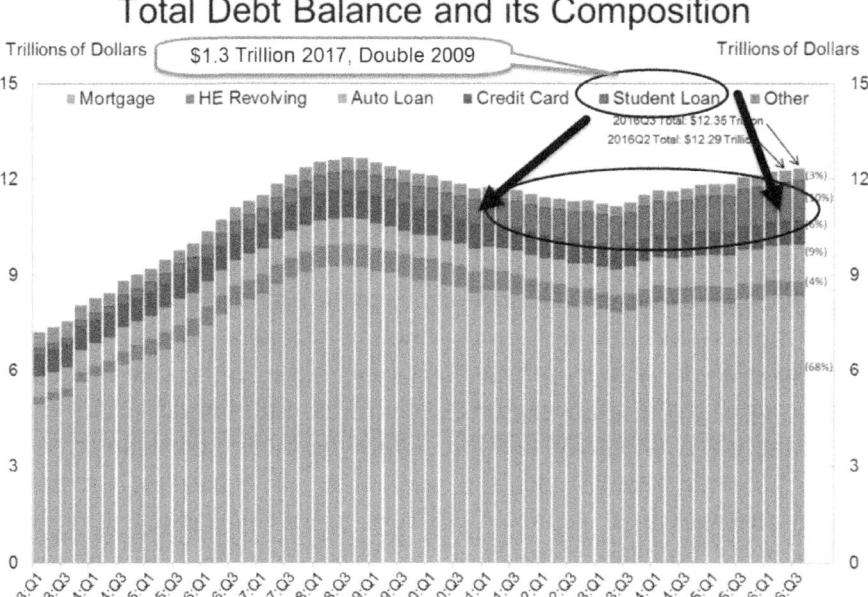

Government to the Rescue

"Politics is the art of looking for trouble, finding it everywhere, diagnosing it incorrectly and applying the wrong remedies."

—Groucho Marx

Getting Political for a Moment

How is it that these congressmen keep getting away with putting us deeper and deeper into debt without repercussions? How is it they can be bought and paid for to the tune of millions of dollars by any industry that wants favors? This is the flaw in our system. If they were

[14] https://www.newyorkfed.org/medialibrary/interactives/householdcredit/data/pdf/HHDC_2016Q3.pdf

held accountable for their actions and weren't allowed to take bribes, and lived within their taxable means except for emergencies, then possibly we wouldn't be in this mess we're in with over $20 trillion in debt. You must understand this is not a left versus right issue. This is an American problem and choosing a new Republican or Democrat leader every 4 or 8 years doesn't change a thing when it comes to spending. You know the data presented here isn't made up and you now know monetary history. You know what the government has done to our money and many of you have benefited from what the government has done and that's just fine. Many with 401k's believe they are wealthy at present from the exact polices our government has conducted. But can they hold onto their wealth? Do they have insurance if things don't go to plan?

You see over and over politicians lie and say whatever their side wants to hear to get elected but once elected there simply is not one fiscal bone in either party when they can print money or borrow (credit) from your children's and grandchildren's future. How do you think millennials and future generations feel about this?

The media by the way is complicit in this, the media tries to keep our minds busy arguing left vs. right issues, racism issues, gay vs. straight vs transgender, marriage issues, abortion and anti-abortion issues, environmental issues etc., (I'm not choosing sides here but explain media tactics) all the while keeping us distracted from what's really going on; the destruction of our economy, our monetary system and thus our nation (now you see the underlying issues that no one discusses anywhere in the media). Its death by 1000 cuts but most can't see they are bleeding. It's the frog in the boiling pot of hot water saying it's warm in here but everything's just fine.

That sounds harsh, but I'm not a fear mongering writer. I am a realist. I can see both sides and profit too because I've done my homework on this. So technically I don't really care what happens in the economy as I know I can move my money to where it grows. That's what the Illusions of Wealth book can help you with. That's a plug for the book, sure, but I just think it can help you beyond what the gold insurance this book recommends for you. Who else is putting the pieces together for you? Your financial advisor who says, trust in stocks? Probably. But take heed in the words of Sun Tzu here; *The general who wins the battle makes many calculations in his temple before the battle is fought. The general who loses makes but few calculations beforehand. Sun Tzu*

My books are about making many calculations in this battle to keep and grow your wealth and I'll continue to write more.

When we keep electing officials that keep putting us further and further in debt (it really doesn't matter if they are Republican or Democrat when it comes to debt/spending), we act like Homer Simpson does and stick our finger in the light socket, get shocked, and stick it in again expecting a different result. But most of us are powerless to do anything about it. If we rose up to do anything about it, the media labels us and tries to put each group against each other when all groups should be pushing our Congressmen and women to pass legislation to stop destroying our futures. But naturally this will never happen. Remember, I am a realist. So, some insurance in gold and silver may make sense. I'm presently addressing this issue with my political book I have been working on 13 years now and finally coming out soon; We the Serfs! (see how the title fits?) In fact, I was going to name that book "Fed Up!" until Texas Governor Rick Perry stole the title.

"First they ignore you, then they laugh at you, then they fight you, then you win."

—Mahatma Gandhi

What is true though is this economy has benefited from government spending. Maybe not for all as the number of homeless is skyrocketing. But understand that the same will hold true for President Trump who funded his empire with debt. However, he declared bankruptcy when he messed up and got to start over again. The U.S. government can't do that. We know electing a new Congress and President won't make a difference every 2 or 4 years, so what comes next?

Charles Lindbergh in 1913 explains this pattern quite well as he warned of what would come.

Carnegie, the Rockefellers, the late Jay Gould, E.H. Harriman and J.P. Morgan, and most of those who have individually amassed wealth by the hundreds of millions, began with little or nothing in the way of capital, except their ability, and the system which permitted their enormous accumulations.

Our government, which is of our own creation, has insured to the banks and other trusts a system which renders it easy for them to oppress the masses. It enables the few to live as non-producers and exorbitant spenders, while almost the entire burden falls on the rest of us. Such a condition is impossible of long tolerance by the proud, honest and intelligent citizens of our country. We must seek for a remedy.[15]

If Lindbergh knew how things would end up and warned about them way back in 1913, the year the Federal Reserve was created, there isn't anyone who is sitting in Congress that would raise a voice warning of what may come. Why would they? They get rich from the cozy relationships they have with big business and the debt marches on with no mention ever by CNBC or other financial media. Ever calculate the interest payment on $20 trillion? It's expected to be $333 billion for 2018. That's more than the entire GDP of Denmark. In 8 short years the interest payment is projected to be more than all but 17 countries in the world. That's if things go as planned and no wars break out or any crisis unfolds (Crisis on average come about once every 9 years and we are about due for one soon). [16,17]

---

[15] Banking and Currency and The Money Trust, Charles A. Lindbergh, 1913, PP. 158-160
http://books.google.com/books?id=B9IZAAAAYAAJ&printsec=frontcover&dq=Banking+and+Currency+and+the+Money+Trust&source=bl&ots=TWgfrqilvu&sig=ZBCX_1a7oa1991JV6GWj5DnVOZM&hl=en&ei=sQAlTL7zOsWqlAfLqtz1Ag&sa=X&oi=book_result&ct=result&resnum=1&ved=0CBUQ6AEwAA#v=onepage&q=j.p.%20morgan&f=false

[16] https://www.thebalance.com/interest-on-the-national-debt-4119024

[17] http://statisticstimes.com/economy/countries-by-projected-gdp.php

How the Expansion Has Evolved – The Best Of Times

If you had an extra $100,000 to spend right now, and didn't have to pay it back for a long time because you had a very low borrowing rate, close to zero percent, would you enjoy yourself and make some purchases of things that make you happy? Go on a trip? Buy a new car or remodel the house? And after that spending spree died down after a few years as the money disappears, you receive another $100,000 that doesn't have to be paid back for a long time. The cycle repeats, but this time a different trip, car and maybe a second home.

That's how our government works.

Our government prints money out of thin air or allows banks to as we alluded to earlier in this book. Their ability to do so is how a private institution like the Federal Reserve makes their money. They make it by Congress' borrowing from them and their infatuation for spending, with no checks and balances as they vote to continually raise the debt ceiling. Some of that printed money goes to individuals and entities that put it to work in markets and push stock prices up to one high after another. This can last forever, right? What can go wrong? Government is always going to be there for us, right?

Well, we all know the fun wouldn't last forever if an individual were to practice this kind of spending, as the individual's credit limit would be maxed out and credit rating decreased to where they wouldn't be able to secure more credit as we discussed earlier. But for our government, it doesn't work that way. They think they can borrow forever and have zero consequences for such borrowing because of that printing press they have, and a complicit banking and Federal Reserve System that will do everything in their power to survive. Who gets hurt in a system like this remains to be seen, but we already saw in 2008/2009 who the U.S. leaders chose to save; the banks.

The National Debt

You don't hear much talk from the financial media, politicians or for that matter anyone regarding the National Debt. This is what we have borrowed from future generations to fund the current and past over spending by Congress.

The total US National Debt is presently over $20 trillion. This debt amounts to just over $60,000 per person in the U.S. and almost $170,000 per tax payer (remember, not everyone pays taxes in the U.S.).[18]

How does this relate to gold? Historically we have seen the national debt move up with the price of gold. The more we spend money we don't have, the higher the price of gold goes. But since about 2011, something happened. The gold price has not followed the debt higher as you can see from the following chart. So, what does it mean? Can debt go up in perpetuity with no consequences? Or is the gold price somehow being suppressed? Which is more logical based on history?

---

[18] http://www.usdebtclock.org/

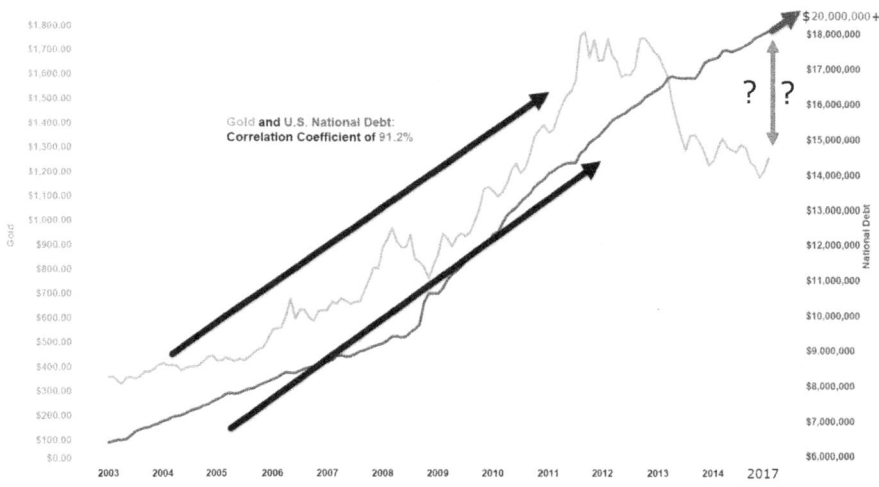

Government Out of Control Spending Benefits the Wealthy

Indeed, what our government and politicians have done is create policy that benefits one group, the wealthy elitists, at the expense of the other, most hard-working Americans.

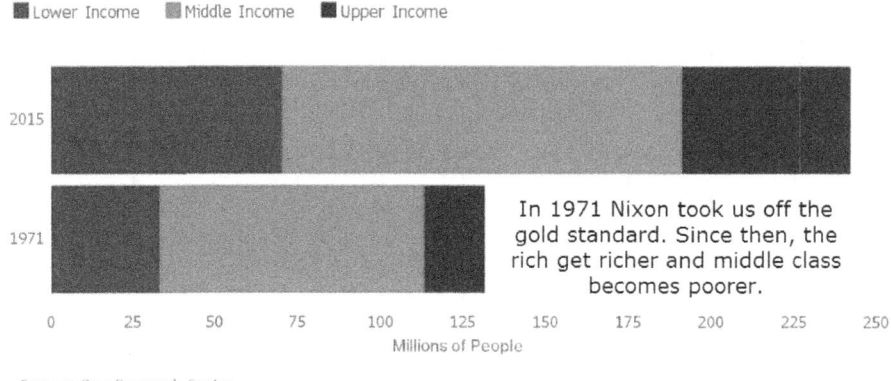

In 1971 Nixon took us off the gold standard. Since then, the rich get richer and middle class becomes poorer.

Source: Pew Research Center

"The Constitution is not an instrument for the government to restrain the people, it is an instrument for the people to

restrain the government - lest it come to dominate our lives and interests."—Patrick Henry

Wages Are Not Increasing

While the government tax receipts keep going higher, even with the Trump administration tax cuts going into effect, wages fell and only recently rose because of minimum wage increases going into effect.[19] Business owners are forced to make decisions; cut back on work hours or accept that profits will fall the higher wages go without real growth. That or turn to artificial intelligence to replace human labor which many companies and even fast food restaurants are turning to. Also, if the unemployment rate into 2018 is so low, then why are non-farm workers earnings growing at only 2.5% annually compared to 4% the last time jobless rates were this low? Globalization and low inflation may be among the reasons.[20]

---

[19] What's Up with U.S. Wage Growth and Job Mobility?
https://www.imf.org/external/pubs/ft/wp/2016/wp16122.pdf

[20] Unemployment in the US is Falling
https://www.bloomberg.com/news/articles/2017-05-19/unemployment-in-the-u-s-is-falling-so-why-isn-t-pay-rising

Doug Eberhardt

Wage Growth Lags the Recovery

Joblessness in the U.S. has fallen sharply from its recession-era peak, but that hasn't accelerated average hourly earnings growth.

UNEMPLOYMENT AND WAGE FIGURES SEASONALLY ADJUSTED
GRAPHIC BY BLOOMBERG BUSINESSWEEK
DATA: BUREAU OF LABOR STATISTICS

Credit Contraction and Deflation

If Americans ever allow banks to control the issue of their currency, first by inflation and then by deflation, the banks will deprive the people of all property until their children will wake up homeless.

—Thomas Jefferson

The quote by Thomas Jefferson above comes to reality if you ever saw the number of homeless in California along the Santa Anita river basin that have recently been kicked out or of those in Los Angeles and San Diego where the number of homeless is rising. Some of these homeless are children where 1 in 10 ages 18-25 are homeless according to a Chapin Hill study over 2 years.[21]

Inflation or Deflation First?

There's a discussion among some people as to whether we will experience inflation from the massive printing and spending by Congress, or if the credit contraction and resulting deflation will swallow any future monetary stimulus.

Before we go any further we must understand a bit more about what deflation means so bear with this section as it is key to understanding what is coming next for the economy, before inflation sets in.

Austrian School economist Jesús Huerta de Soto presents Three Types of Deflation:

1. The first type consists of policies adopted by public authorities to deliberately reduce the quantity of money in circulation. This whole process of deliberate deflation contributes nothing and merely subjects the economic system to unnecessary pressure.
2. The second type of deflation, which should be clearly distinguished from the first, occurs when economic agents decide to save; that is, to refrain from consuming a significant portion of their income and to devote all or part of the monetary total saved to increasing their cash balances (i.e. hoarding). In this case, the rise in the demand for money tends to push up the purchasing power of the monetary unit (the dollar).
3. The third type of deflation we will consider results from the tightening of credit which normally occurs in the crisis and recession stage that follows all credit expansion. Just as credit expansion increases the quantity of money in circulation, the massive repayment of loans and the loss of value

[21] http://voicesofyouthcount.org/wp-content/uploads/2017/11/ChapinHall_VoYC_1-Pager_Final_111517.pdf .

> on the asset side of banks' balance sheets, both caused by the crisis, trigger an inevitable, cumulative process of credit tightening which reduces the quantity of money in circulation (and credit) and thus generates deflation. This third type of deflation arises when, as the crisis is emerging, not only does credit expansion stop increasing, but there is actually a credit squeeze and thus, deflation, or a drop in the money supply, or quantity of money in circulation.

The second and primarily third definition fit what I see coming for the U.S. economy, a deflationary credit contraction. Congress that refuses to implement the necessary austerity measures to reduce the debt. Quantitative easing has done nothing but increase the risk with the Fed's balance sheet in their quest to prevent deflation or a contraction in the economy.

In fact, deflation is not a bad thing to see materialize in the economy. It gets rid of the bad debt and can get the economy back on track if there is no interference by government.

Jörg Guido Hülsmann, in his book *Deflation & Liberty*, agrees, stating "there is absolutely no reason to be concerned about the economic effects of deflation—unless one equates the welfare of the nation with the welfare of its false elites. There is absolutely no hope that the Federal Reserve or any other fiat money producer of the world will change their policies any time soon."[22]

This is what's at the heart of this entire chapter. The Federal Reserve has as one of their 2 mandates, to target a 2% inflation rate (the other being full employment). While into 2018 the unemployment rate has been low, the Fed wants inflation. We have already discussed what this 2% inflation does over time. It makes things more expensive.

What policies are implemented to benefit the hard-working laborer in the United States? Indeed, they kick them while they're up with higher taxes and kick them while they're down when they implement stimulus packages to protect the interests of the elite and increasing the national debt rather than let the free market work things out for itself, weeding out what's bad, like the banks that deserved to fail centered

---

[22] Jörg Guido Hülsmann, Deflation & Liberty P. 43

around the 2009 financial crisis. This would have only hurt the few elitists that deserved to be hurt with their carelessness.

This is how Murray Rothbard described a similar experience to where we are today that occurred during the Great Depression: "Deflationary credit contraction greatly helps to speed up the adjustment process, and hence the completion of business recovery."[23]

Government is always trying to combat any credit contraction with record borrowing, again, no matter who is in control of the White House or Congress. The Debt-to-GDP ratio keeps moving higher and higher and is currently over 104% as the following chart shows.

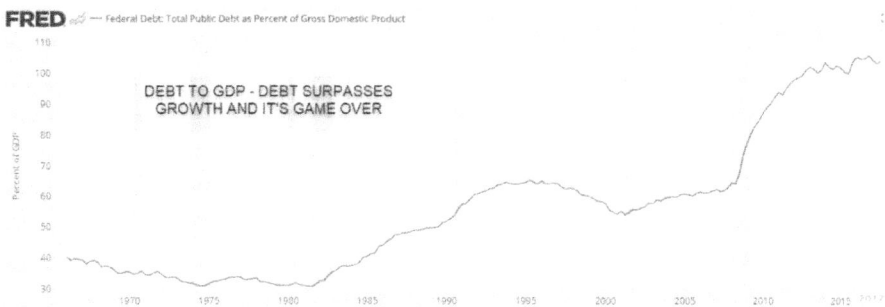

As an example of what is likely to occur here in the U.S. in the future we turn to what has being going on in Japan which is experiencing its decades of deflation. Japan's GDP as a percentage of debt has risen to 229% with no end in sight or solutions for that matter.

---

[23] America's Great Depression, Murray N. Rothbard, 1963 P. 17

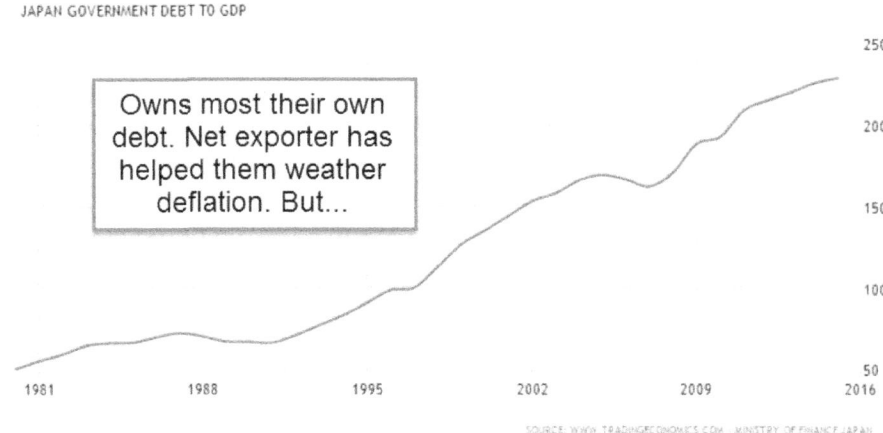

You can see where Japan and the U.S. are compared to the rest of the world as they are leaders when it comes to their share of global debt.[24]

---

[24] http://www.visualcapitalist.com/63-trillion-world-debt-one-visualization/

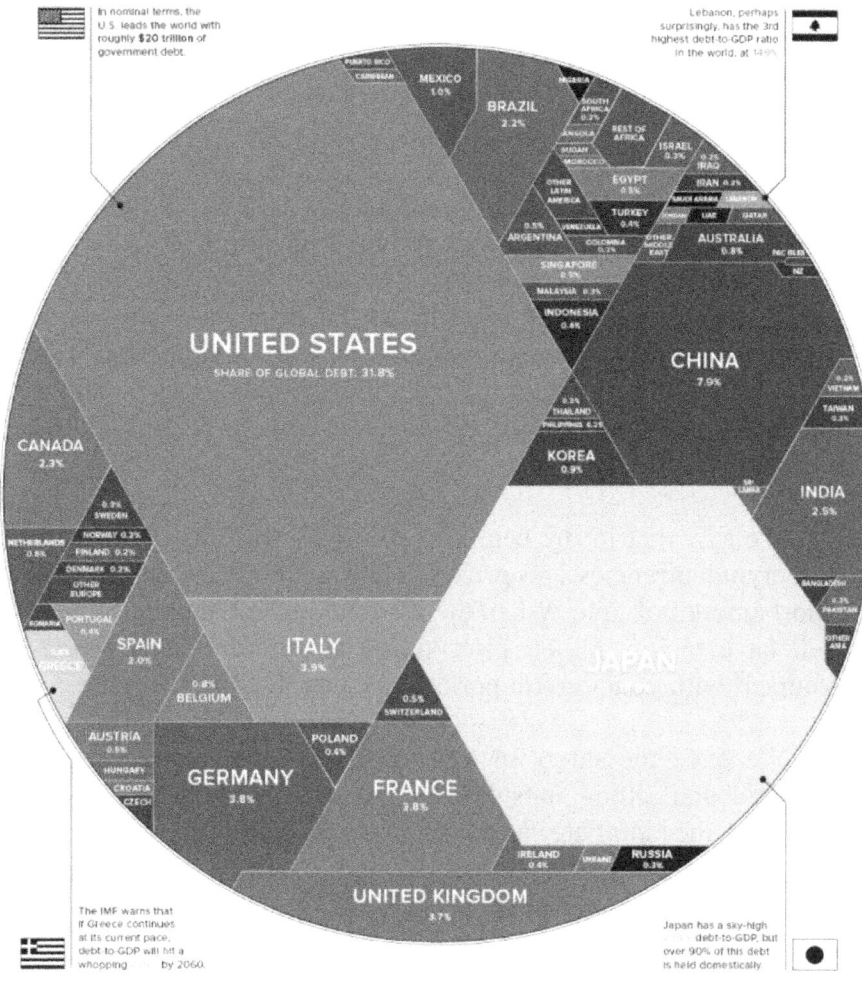

How A Deflationary Credit Contraction Will Unfold

Visually, this deflationary credit contraction can be shown in an upside-down pyramid first formalized from the economist we spoke of earlier, John Exter. He first came up with the inverse pyramid in the 1970s when we first started seeing credit grow. From Reagan to Trump, it has kept growing to the tune of 100's of trillions when you consider derivatives. The riskiest assets sit on top of the pyramid and they funnel down in search of safety as the deflation escalates. Today's assets are not what they were in the 70's but the concept is still the same. The contraction causes wealth to seek liquidity and if there are no buyers, then prices are lowered of assets across the board, with the riskiest assets possibly not having any buyers at all and in risk of default.

We saw that in the beginning of 2018 with the first real crash of the cryptocurrencies and prices falling as much as 50% or more in a short amount of time. When there are no buyers, those who do want to sell have to lower their price more and more. The question to ask yourself with your current portfolio is, how liquid are they?

We have the safety of treasuries and cash at the bottom of the pyramid and sitting outside the pyramid are gold and silver which embody the ultimate level of trust because of their history of maintaining purchasing power but just as important the fact they are the only asset that is **no one else's liability**.

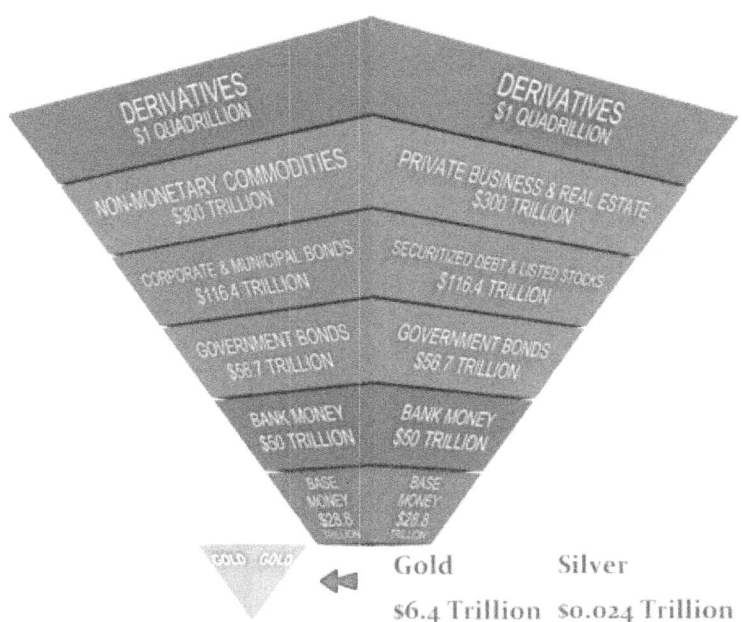

Richard Koo describes this debt deflation as a "balance sheet recession," which is also the name of his 2003 book describing the Japanese deflation.

> The problem is that a balance sheet recession is no ordinary recession. In this recession, which is brought about by the fallacy of composition, the economy is weakening because most companies are looking backward as they try to repair their balance sheets. But because the companies are minimizing debt instead of maximizing profits, demand is lost all around the economy. If no one came in to fill the shortfall in demand created by everyone paying down debt, the whole economy could fall into a vicious cycle.[25]

While this synopsis was written in 2003, we are seeing it play out in the U.S. as corporations have been buying back shares to make their

---

[25] Balance Sheet Recession, Richard C. Koo, 2003 P. 231

profit look better. Even Japan's exports have declined 13 straight months all the while Japan's leaders have lowered the value of the yen. Yet in both cases for the U.S. and Japan, the stock market shot straight up during this time. It's a fake stock market if you ask me, but it doesn't mean one can't profit from it. One can also lock in some of that profit if they see trouble ahead for the economy.

We've experienced this episode of deflation here in the U.S. before in the beginning years of the Great Depression. Rothbard describes: "Hardest hit, in accordance with Austrian cycle theory, were producers' goods and higher-order capital goods industries, rather than the consumer goods industries. Thus, from the end of 1929 to the end of 1931, the FRB index of production of durable manufactures fell by over 50%, while the index of non-durable production fell by less than 20%."[26]

Are we going to be repeating this deleveraging era? What do the statistics today tell us?

Bill Gross of PIMCO sums this up quite well. He states, "Investors must respect this rather tortuous journey in the months and years ahead for what it is: A deleveraging process based upon too much debt and too little growth to service it."[27]

The enormous size of this debt, which overwhelms the entire GDP of the country, is revealed in the following chart. Please note the contraction process has just begun, as the Total Credit Market Debt as a % of GDP ratio has fallen from a high of 372.99% to 348.6% by the 3rd quarter 2017, according to data compiled by Ned Davis Research.[28]

---

[26] America's Great Depression, Murray N. Rothbard, 1963, P. 261
[27] Bill Gross June 2010 Investment Outlook PIMCO http://media.pimco-global.com/pdfs/pdf/IO%20June%202010%20WEB.pdf?WT.cg_n=PIMCO-US&WT.ti=IO%20June%202010%20WEB.pdf
[28] **Copyright 2018 Ned Davis Research, Inc. Further distribution prohibited without prior permission. All Rights Reserved.**

See NDR Disclaimer at www.ndr.com/copyright.html. **For data vendor disclaimers refer to** www.ndr.com/vendorinfo/.

Buy Gold and Silver Safely

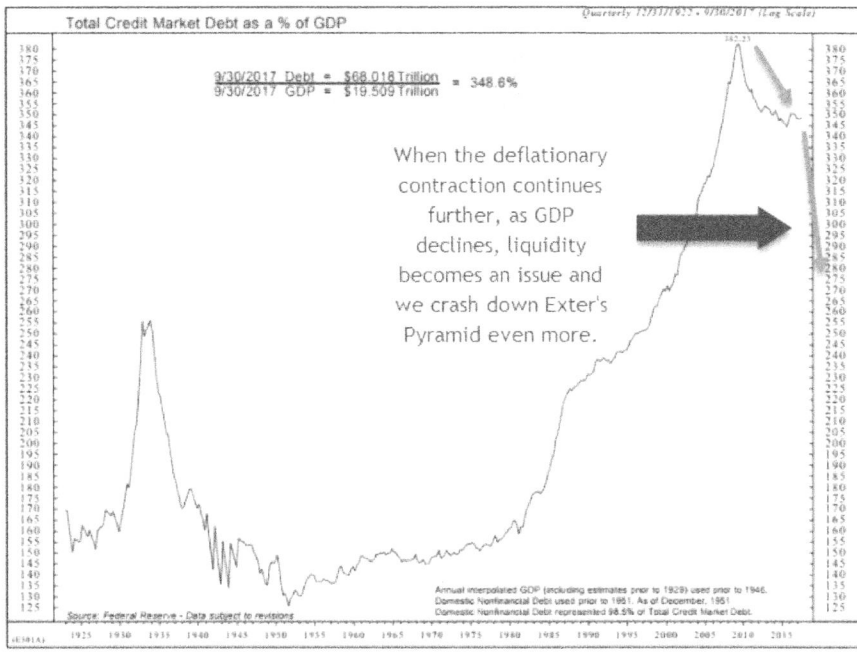

Capital flows down the pyramid and assets that were propped up on credit (leverage) could end up with no bid (buyers) and even default. Many assets will suffer as they are not liquid enough to handle the mass request for withdrawals without subjecting themselves to even further decline. Based on the chart, this contraction has already started and it's the story no one is talking about in the financial media (along with the story about Debt over 20.6 trillion. We have seen several examples of this issue of mass withdrawals recently during what is perceived as one of the strongest markets in history.

Third Avenue Focused Credit Fund suffered almost $1 billion in redemptions in 2015 and finally had to stop redemptions and close on Dec. 9, 2015. The high yield fund had $3.5 billion at one time. As funds flowed out, the managers of the fund risk selling assets in a market that would push prices down lower and hurting remaining investors in the fund.[29]

Tudor Fund had $1 billion in redemptions in 2017 after 3 years of lackluster returns and it was considered one of the oldest and well regarded in the industry.[30]

Six property funds in the UK halted redemptions in 2016 as asset managers came under pressure to sell buildings in order to raise cash.[31]

Some of you think you are wealthy because you own a nice piece of real estate or some other assets that have appreciated nicely. If you ever needed money you might be able to borrow against the asset, but during a deflationary contraction, there may not be any lending. Worse case one may have to sell the asset to raise the needed cash. Many just aren't as liquid as you think they are. It may make sense to think about liquidating now, before the coming contraction, especially if you will need funds anytime soon. Even those close to retirement and planning on selling their home may want to downsize sooner into a smaller place and use the extra proceeds from the sale to live off of. You will be in a situation in the future where you wish you would have. Cycles work that way.

Other issues that can come to fruition are your property taxes could increase as state governments look for ways to pay their bills like increasing demands of pensions for government employees. You also have upkeep expenses on an aging house like a new roof, furnace, air conditioning, paint, etc. and that gets expensive, especially if inflation kicks in. And when it comes time to sell, what will the demand be? Where will the buyers come from for your home, especially if it is larger and more expensive? Who will afford the monthly mortgage when rates shoot up? In 2018 there was already tax code changes that caused higher end property owners the ability to deduct mortgage interest they were accustomed to deducting.

[29] Third Avenue Plans to Liquidate Focused Credit Fund After Losses
https://www.bloomberg.com/news/articles/2015-12-10/third-avenue-plans-to-liquidate-focused-credit-fund-after-losses

[30] Tudor Investors Ask to Pull more than 1 Billion from Firm
https://www.bloomberg.com/news/articles/2016-04-14/tudor-investors-ask-to-pull-more-than-1-billion-from-firm

[31] https://www.ft.com/content/69e8b476-4389-11e6-9b66-0712b3873ae1

There are many things to consider as to what wealth really is. If you are relying on equity in your house to tap for income in the future, you might want to make a move to sell sooner than later or at a minimum downsize to the area you want to be the rest of your life if not where you are presently.

Even your pension can be attacked as many companies find out that the money is just not there to take care of everyone. Pensions struggle today to make payouts and we have had the best years of the stock market ever. And this is again during one of the best stock market runs of all time. Companies have cut back on health coverage and you'll see more and more pensions cut back their payouts to retirees as well in the years to come "to save the system" for all other retirees. It's already a mess in places like Illinois. What happens when the next recession hits? What if it is a severe recession? What are the odds based on what is written in this book? Have I just made up statistics or are the facts presented to make a case for some insurance that gold and silver offer?

If you don't believe this can happen because you have a government job, look no further than Illinois and their inability to fund public employee pensions which are only 37.6% funded and a current shortfall of $250 billion. The alternative is not pay you at all, but more than likely a reduction in promises must occur. That's not going to make those in or close to retirement so happy and as an investor who is contemplating retiring with a pension, some insurance in assets outside your pension makes sense. I also address this in my Illusions of Wealth book (another illusion unfortunately for those who were promised one thing but may get some surprises related to their retirement instead). This goes for Social Security as well as they keep increasing the age for eligibility and tax more of your income!

The government is never going to be in your best interest, only theirs. That's why my next book We the Serfs! exploits these kings and queens who take from us to enrich themselves, all the while turning us more and more into serfs to serve their needs. That's not what this country stands for and you can bet any issues you just heard above are coming and many of you won't be prepared. Don't assume all is well. Be proactive with your investing and retirement. Plan ahead with some insurance as well found in gold and silver at the bottom of the pyramid as they are the only "real" asset that can't be abused by government.

Velocity of Money

There are other signs that not all is well that support a deflationary credit contraction. You can see that money is not flowing in the economy but mostly being hoarded. Remember, consumers make up 70% of GDP with their spending, but you can see that money velocity, the number of times money is spent to buy goods and service over a period of time, has been decreasing every year.

Another sign of this slowdown can be found in the Baltic Dry Sea Index, which shows a very steep decline.[32] The Index provides price analysis of the various cost of moving raw materials like iron ore, coal, building materials and grains, not just in the Baltic Sea, but across many shipping routes in the world. As you can see, leading up to 2009 there was a decent amount of activity, but since then it hardly looks like a recovery is going on, despite the S&P 500 hitting record highs.

---

[32] Baltic Dry Index Chart from Investment Tools
http://investmenttools.com/futures/bdi_baltic_dry_index.htm

The second chart shows this disconnect and adds to the case of the coming deflationary contraction that can hit stocks hard.

Turning the Monetary System Upside Down

Knowing whether one will be able to convert what they perceive as wealth to something of intrinsic value (money) is the important factor to consider when thinking about acquiring gold. Our Founding Fathers knew the value of gold and silver when they created the Constitution in the late 18th century. It seems that allowing the Federal Reserve to take over our monetary system by substituting FRNs in their place has brought us full circle.

All we citizens want is a medium of exchange that represents our ability to transact purchases and pay wages. It is the government and the Federal Reserve that have turned things upside down.

One important caveat to consider, however, is what economist Frank Shostak says about the two types of credit: "Contrary to popular thinking, it is not a fall in credit as such that is the key to deflation, but a fall specifically in credit created out of thin air. It is this type of credit, which commercial banks have created through fractional-reserve lending, that causes the decline in money supply, i.e., deflation. A fall in normal credit (i.e., credit that has an original lender) doesn't alter the money supply, and hence has nothing to do with deflation."[33]

Indeed, it is the banking system we need to look at next, as the health of the banking system, in conjunction with the monetary system, is an important issue to analyze.

Banking Crisis

All the above analysis needs to include a look at the U.S. banking system. Without its stability, we end up with a monetary system problem that can possibly lead to hyperinflation. That's why you saw in the last financial crisis, the ones who run the show do all they can to save the banks.

Banks for a time slowed down with their risk taking as legislation called the Dodd Frank Wall Street Reform and Consumer Protection Act was passed to curtail their derivative activity that caused many banks to get in trouble during the last crisis. But after 10 great years in the stock market and no fear of any issues with banks arising since the Federal Reserve and Congress helped bail them out, Congress is now already looking to roll back many or all of Dodd-Frank as the House already voted to do this. It's no surprise. Today banks continually make decisions as a whole that lead to multi-million-dollar lawsuits and Congress wants to cut them more slack. This is what leads to

---

[33] Does a Fall in Credit Lead to Deflation? by Frank Shostak, October 29, 2009 http://mises.org/daily/3810

issues and always will. Banks know the government has their back should they mess up again. This is called moral hazard. They have impunity and they know it. So, they will always take on more risk.

This brings us to news from the Wall Street Journal that leveraged loans are booming in the U.S. once again. In fact, volumes have risen 53% in 2017 and are on track to surpass the 534B record in 2003. According to the Journal, "The recent Toys R Us bankruptcy filing is a prime example of a company that had piled on too much debt. According to the WSJ, a large portion of the $5.3B it had accumulated was made up of leveraged loans and high-yield bonds."[34] As early as late 2015 regulators have been condemning lending practices at US banks and don't seem to be slowing down.[35]

One area to keep an eye on the additional risk they take on is the Office of the Comptroller of the Currency Quarterly Report on Bank Trading and Derivatives Activities. Four major banks with the most derivative activity hold 89.6% of all derivatives; JP Morgan, Citibank, Bank of America and Goldman Sachs. But the interconnection of banks today shows that if one has issues, most all will have issues and this quarterly report needs to be monitored to see if trouble is on the horizon.[36]

Summary

To summarize this chapter, we realize the stock market has moved to record highs and pullback are always inevitable. The easy credit since

---

[34] http://www.abfjournal.com/dailynews/wsj-leveraged-loans-on-pace-to-top-pre-crisis-records/

[35] https://www.bisnow.com/national/news/capital-markets/banks-to-fed-weve-tightened-commercial-real-estate-lending-59756

[36] https://www.occ.gov/topics/capital-markets/financial-markets/derivatives/derivatives-quarterly-report.html

the early 80's and the expansion of wealth in the U.S. has made many rich, but at a cost to the entire monetary system as when interest rates rise this will all be revealed. We have a fractional reserve monetary system and a Federal Reserve System that allows for money to be created out of thin air, and a Congress that can't stop spending. Is it any wonder this type of system would get abused at some point?

Growth isn't what it used to be, and the consumer is already feeling the pinch with more and more credit card delinquencies. The National Debt is over $20 Trillion and the contraction of all these years of excesses is unavoidable. Economist John Exter predicted it before we even got to the levels we have attained today. We'll likely see future banking crisis' and the Federal Reserve apply the wrong medicine once again to "save the system" instead of letting the entities that make the wrong decisions fail and weed out the bad in the economy. We never let that happen in 2009 and banks are back at it again taking on more risk and the Federal Reserve's balance sheet is still a mess. What you need to ask is "what if" the Fed and Congress, who both missed the last crisis, really don't have their act together and the tools necessary to fend off a future recession or worse? Then ask yourself, based on what's written in this chapter, what makes you think they do have the tools necessary? And could this time really be different? And how are you prepared and protected financially?

Chapter 5
Common Objections to Buying Gold

Gold Is Not a Good Inflation Hedge

Many of those who critique gold, do so when comparing it as an inflation hedge, but then cherry pick dates to compare gold to how inflation has performed. For example, they will use a high price for gold historically, like the 1980 high of $850 or the 2011 closing high of $1,917 and say that some other asset like stocks has easily outperformed gold. The whole thought of gold as a good inflation hedge changes when you use a year like 1971 when Nixon took us off the gold standard. Any comparison before that is irrelevant because the price of gold was fixed from 1935 until 1971. Also, the demand aspects of gold by individuals have been skewed even after 1971 because Americans could only purchase $100 of gold before 1975. 1975 is a good year to start any analysis comparing gold to another asset and at that time it averaged $161.02 per ounce. In reality though, just looking at the big picture, there are times to own gold and times not to. That's what cycles dictate. If that stock market is at record highs, do asset allocation models dictate you put money in stocks or an asset that has been beaten down like gold/silver?

One could also use the year 2000 when the Euro came into existence to show the strength of gold as the dollar finally had other competition to it. Gold took off as the dollar fell.

Gold Is Just a Shiny Rock

Gold is a metal, not a rock, as we discussed previously.[1]

---

[1] http://www.chemicalelements.com/elements/au.html

Basic Information

Name: Gold
Symbol: Au
Atomic Number: 79
Atomic Mass: 196.96655 amu
Melting Point: 1064.43 °C (1337.5801 K, 1947.9741 °F)
Boiling Point: 2807.0 °C (3080.15 K, 5084.6 °F)
Number of Protons/Electrons: 79
Number of Neutrons: 118
Classification: Transition Metal
Crystal Structure: Cubic
Density @ 293 K: 19.32 g/cm^3
Color: Gold

Gold Is a Speculative Investment

There are times to own gold and there are times to sell gold. There are times to own stocks and there are times to sell stocks. The same goes for bonds, real estate, oil and many other investments. But history has shown gold to be the best medium of exchange or money and over time maintains its purchasing power. There is nothing speculative about that, but it does give many investors peace of mind. It is very liquid which many of the others are not as well.

You Can't Eat Gold

You can't eat your Apple, Amazon, Google (aka; Alphabet Inc.) or Facebook stock either. But you can convert each of these and gold to the scrip of the day; dollars.

In Armageddon You Want Guns and Food, Not Gold

This is true. Survival is what is most important in a Mad Max kind of world. But who do you think would be running this world and own the guns and food distribution centers? The old saying, "he who has the gold makes the rules." The gold hoarder would have sold his gold or exchanged it for guns long before Armageddon when the economy devolves to barter. While still available, the gold investor, because they are forward thinking and prepare for the worst-case scenario, is the type of person who would stock up on anything they needed to ride out the apocalypse. Those who say gold is useless in times of Armageddon don't give the owner of gold credit for thinking about the future. Gold bugs probably think about the future more than anyone else.

Gold Is a Lousy Investment

Gold is insurance against a falling or potentially failing currency. In the U.S. that currency is the dollar or Federal Reserve Note. Gold is money, not an investment. But sure, at times it is a great investment and at times a lousy investment. But over time, it maintains purchasing power. Its value can never go to zero and you can't say that about any other investment. It is insurance that will be there when you need it most. When the financial crisis potentially comes, government will restrict withdrawals from your bank ATM. We have already seen this in many countries like Greece for example. When everyone else is trying to get their maximum allotment government from their bank accounts via the ATM, gold investors have the upper hand and can still barter with real money.

Stocks Are a Better Investment Than Gold

No doubt stocks have done well over time. But comparing gold to an individual stock or even an index is not a fair comparison. The Dow Jones Industrial Average in 1896 used to consist of just 12 company stocks, not the 30 it consists of today. But look at the changes over time with these companies. What exists today may not be the same tomorrow.

- **American Cotton Oil** – Ancestor of Best Foods, now part of Unilever.
- **American Sugar** – Became Amstar in 1970 and subsequently Domino Foods.
- **American Tobacco** – Broke up into separate businesses in 1911, expanded beyond tobacco and renamed itself American Brands; now Fortune Brands.
- **Chicago Gas** – Absorbed by Peoples Gas, which replaced it in the Dow in 1898. Now part of Integrys Energy.
- **Distilling & Cattle Feeding** – After a series of deals became National Distillers, then sold liquor assets to Diageo and fellow Dow component progeny American Brands. Rest of business now part of Millennium Chemicals.
- **General Electric** –Still an independent company with diversified assets around the world. Was removed from the Dow twice around the turn of the 20th century, but was reinstated both times.
- **Laclede Gas** – Still around, as the primary subsidiary of the Laclede Group.
- **National Lead** – Changed its name to NL Industries in 1971, 83% owned by conglomerate Valhi. Once known for mining, moved into paints (Dutch Boy brand), pigments and coatings. Sold paint business in 1970s.
- **North American** – Dissolved by a federal court in 1938, surviving successor became Wisconsin Electric, part of Wisconsin Energy.
- **Tennessee Coal Iron and RR** – During the panic of 1907, TC&I was acquired by U.S. steel, with banker J.P. Morgan playing a key role in arranging the merger.
- **U.S. Leather** – The only preferred stock in the original Dow, U.S. Leather is also the only company to have vanished with nary a trace since the trust was dissolved in 1911.
- **United States Rubber** – Merged first into Uniroyal in 1950s then with B.F. Goodrich in 1986. Resulting company was bought by France's Michelin in 1990.

(Sources: Dow Jones Indexes, Prof. Richard Sylla, Museum of American Finance.)

Meanwhile, an ounce of gold in 1896 is an ounce of gold today. It never changes.

Stocks are great investments. This book is not about knocking stocks, but yes, I can point out at times when the stock market may be overvalued. Gold is one of the few assets though that can counteract a declining dollar and is a great complement to any portfolio.

Gold Is Too Volatile

No, gold doesn't change. It is the currency that it is priced in that changes.

Gold Has No Intrinsic Value

Neither do diamonds but people buy them all the time for their significant others.

Gold Doesn't Pay Dividends

Again, neither do diamonds, or many stocks. You want income, buy dividend paying stocks but know their value can decline with the stock market and you can lose principal. If you own gold and need to raise cash from an appreciated stash, you can always do so.

Nothing wrong with owning a portfolio that consists of stocks, bonds, dividend paying stocks, tax-free bonds, real estate and precious metals. Asset allocation models can tell you when one is a better buy or a potential sell.

Chapter 6
<u>How Does Gold Fit into A Diversified Portfolio?</u>

Longtime investment newsletter writer and now no longer with us, Richard Russell, was one of the first to introduce gold to me as a must for one's portfolio. In fact, he went so far as to hold 50% of his assets in gold he believed in it so much.

Russell had this to say about the gold:[1]

> I've written in the past that if you want to make 'BIG' money in the market, you have to take an over-sized position and be dead right on the trend. The last time I did that was in late 1958. ... I did extremely well in that fateful ride, and I never again had the nerve to take that large a position–until now.
>
> I started building my gold position in 1999.... My gold position now is comparable to my market position back in 1958. Why have I done this again?
>
> (1) I believe gold is in a major or primary bull market. I believe the gold bull market is currently in its second phase. This is the phase where sophisticated and seasoned investors and the funds enter the market.
> (2) If there is only one bull market in progress, it will attract broad new coverage and attention.
> (3) I believe the bear market in stocks will continue erratically and the deflationary trends will persist. ... Central banks will stop at nothing (including massive printing of dollars) in their effort to halt deflation.

Russell is right about gold being in the 2nd phase of the gold market which we'll address in a moment. But there is no way he could have predicted the massive amount of debt accumulated via credit, not just the physical printing of dollars.

---

[1] Richard Russell, Dow Theory Letters http://www.dowtheoryletters.com

Why has the deflation and bear market in stocks been postponed? Because the government, Fed and Treasury prolonged the recession with more stimulus packages, bailouts and quantitative easing and continued deficit spending after the 2009 crash and that has continued with the surprising victory of Donald Trump as President.

Instead of predictions about where the price of gold will be in the future, which anyone can throw out a number, this book is more about reframing your thinking about real money (gold as opposed to FRNs), the economy, government, media, Congress and the Federal Reserve. Naturally preserving and growing your wealth will come because you have a better understanding of what really is happening in these uncertain economic times that are coming. I say uncertain because when you have a stock market that doesn't pull back, most anyone knows at some point it will. When it does, and interest rates rise hurting bonds, where else besides cash will money flow? That answer is gold. Richard Russell knew this, and he would be saying the same thing today about gold as he did then.

I understand the importance of profiting with stocks. However, many investors are concerned about the stability of the U.S. economy and just want to insure their wealth isn't lost through possible government screw ups. The fact is, governments always screw up. The question to be answered is when will the next screw up come and how is your portfolio prepared for this just in case all the kings horses and all the kings men can't put the humpty dumpty economy back together again when it falls. In fact, as I have mentioned, you are putting your entire faith in your portfolio in the currency that backs it, the U.S. dollar, which has an existence of 47 years without a relationship with gold. Please let that sink in a minute. Most of you reading this are probably older than the dollar's existence without gold and I'm guessing you don't know much about gold either since our schools have neglected to give you the proper history of it as money. Now let it sink in that we have over $20 trillion of debt backing those dollars and unfunded liabilities in the trillions for future payments to Social Security, Medicare, welfare and the military industrial complex.

No matter what the objective of the investor, it's important to understand where we are in this current gold bull market and see if now is a good time to buy gold or to hold off for lower prices. Or, just say to yourself, I really don't trust government and want that insurance and will just buy and hold throughout as I know it's there when I need it. There are many out there that are in this camp and I know because I field the phone calls from them. They simply don't trust government. They don't put all their money in precious metals, but they do feel they have peace of mind when they diversify with some metals.

Richard Russell says there are three phases to a gold bull market:[2]

> First phase is where sophisticated investors, sensing a new bull market, make their initial commitment.
> In the second phase, the public will start to buy gold, this in reaction to increasing political and social uncertainty, rising debt levels and nervousness as to the future of the dollar.

(This is where we are now but in 2016 was delayed a bit with the election of Donald Trump – but this won't matter as he loves debt as much as anyone and went so far as to say we don't need a debt ceiling as I mentioned. When you work in debt your entire life by securing loans for properties, you make the assumption that real estate will always go higher, and the loan will take care of itself. Congress and President Trump are convinced that the economy will always grow, and the debt will become less of a problem if we concentrate on growing the economy, especially with the gifts corporations have received with lower taxes. But we've already seen the economy isn't growing over 4% or close to historic data of growth, except for a few starts in certain industries. The potential of a contraction is close to the highest it's ever been. Remember, President Trump has declared bankruptcy in the past and that's something the U.S. elite won't let happen to the U.S. as it would defeat all their goals. They would rather you and your children and children's children pay for their current over spending and live high on the hog today.)

---

[2] Ibid

> The third phase of the gold bull market will see a frantic rush by the public to buy gold. In this phase, gold will surge to undreamed of heights– a level beyond what anyone now envisions.

We have seen bitcoin go to undreamed of heights in early 2018, then in a week crashed 50%. All assets have cycle blow off tops. Real estate did leading up to the last crisis and now looks to be topping in the expensive New York area again. But bitcoin and real estate haven't experienced central banks manipulating the price like they have with their gold sales agreements. While banks around the world in South Korea, Australia and India freeze accounts of bitcoin, they are seeing it as a threat to their scheme. But bitcoin isn't a physical asset like gold that banks can get their hands on and make it disappear in value. This can be good or bad and still in its infancy. But all central banks still hold gold as I said to keep the illusion it actually backs the dollars you hold.

Central bankers aren't the smartest bunch. When gold finally does enter this 3rd stage, it is you, the one who has already purchased the gold, that will be in control of the real wealth that only gold can secure for your portfolio. Most everyone else won't know what happened, including Congress and the Fed, just like in 2009.

Do investors have any portfolio insurance? Where do they go to acquire gold? What kind of gold investment should they be making? How much of their portfolio should be allocated to gold? Can an investor put gold in their IRA or invest in gold through their 401(k)?

These and many more questions this book will answer in the coming chapters.

Diversification with Gold

Gold began to take off in price in the year 2000. It had 10 years in a row of moving higher and began to decline when the dollar started to rebound again. The stock market began to take off and gold fell and with the stock market taking off, many investors simply ignored gold. But an interesting thing occurred during those years of the gold decline. My company has been selling gold since the year 2010 and most everyone who purchased metals have not sold it back to us. This tells me the psychology of the buyer of gold is one where they view gold more as insurance than as a get rich quick type of investment.

What I recommend is diversifying your portfolio with insurance. I understand some of you may view gold as an investment, and yes, it does reduce volatility overall for one's portfolio when you add gold to it, but you must realize what I said earlier, that there isn't much in your portfolio that can counteract the dollar risk. Gold is the best asset to do this and most don't own it.

How Does Gold Help Improve Portfolio Performance?

The biggest test for gold in the last decade came in 2008/2009, when stock markets across the world were plummeting. Gold lost some of its luster during this decline, as banks, mutual funds and hedge funds were liquidating the only asset they could to accommodate the panic withdrawals of their clients and the dollar shot up as investors wanted stability. But even money markets had some issues back then with the net asset value of one going below $1 for the first time. However, gold still managed to end the year of the crisis with a gain while the stock markets of the world kept falling through March of 2009.

According to a paper, *Is Gold a Hedge or a Safe Haven? An Analysis of Stocks, Bonds and Gold*, written by Dirk G. Baur, School of Finance and Economics, University of Technology and Brian M. Lucey, School of Business, Trinity College Dublin:[3]

> "Gold is a safe haven for investors if either stocks or bonds fall. Gold is a hedge against stocks and is a contemporaneous safe haven in extreme

---

[3] Dirk G. Baur and Brian M. Lucey paper, "Is Gold a Hedge or a Safe Haven? An Analysis of Stocks, Bonds and Gold" June 2007
http://www.tcd.ie/iiis/documents/discussion/pdfs/iiisdp198.pdf

stock market conditions. Gold is a hedge at all times, that is, including gold in a portfolio increases the degree of diversification.

Since the price of gold increases when stock prices fall in the U.S., gold has the potential to compensate investors for losses with stocks, thereby positively influencing market sentiment and the resiliency of the financial system."

Based on their research, when it came to these "extreme" stock market conditions, people ran to the safe haven of gold. I think we'll see this again once the deflationary credit contraction evolves into inflation and super inflation.

Boom and Bust Cycles

Ryan M. Daly, Client Analyst with Goldman Sachs, wrote a scholarly paper called *Tactical Asset Allocation to Gold*, where he made the point that markets do have their periods where they don't produce positive returns after a period of Federal Reserve credit expansion, such as 1929 and 1965. According to his research, the Dow was basically flat for 25 years from 1929 to 1954, and again for 16 years from 1966 to 1982.[4]

The Dow hit a low in 2009 of 6,547 and through 2018 hit high after high surpassing 26,000 for the first time ever.

During the baseball season of 1998, Sammy Sosa and Mark McGwire were involved in an epic battle to break the season home run record of 61 held by Roger Maris. It was quite enjoyable to watch as they pounded out home run after home run, especially once they passed Maris' record and continued to hit even more home runs. But that season should have an asterisk placed on it with all the steroid use by certain players who were belting the home runs. Without the steroid stimulus, as enjoyable as it was to experience the home run race, the record wouldn't have been broken. The euphoria was tainted, as it wasn't supposed to occur in the first place.

---

[4] Ryan Daly paper, "Tactical Asset Allocation to Gold" May 2005 http://papers.ssrn.com/sol3/papers.cfm?abstract_id=783187

It was the steroid Federal Reserve policies of lower rates that caused the housing boom leading to the last boom, followed by the raising of rates because they thought they were doing the right thing. Instead, they quashed the real estate market, escalated the problems with banks (who need to take some of the blame because they were selling subprime mortgages and heavily involved in the derivatives game. But they did so with a complacent Fed giving them the appearance that the game would last forever. They forgot about cycles. Fast forward to 2018 and we have seen the Fed turn off the quantitative easing but is making the mistake of raising rates when the economy is built on fluff and hope. It's built on the QE stimulus, a quadrupling of the Fed balance sheet, and now banks are playing the derivatives game again. It was built on low rates that the Fed had set and now the Fed is raising rates. Déjà vu anyone? But the Fed is doing this without their stated inflation goals of 2% being met and as I said, Yellen calls this a mystery. If it's a mystery, then why do it? Why not wait for the economy to show more signs of strength, like GDP over 4%? Why raise rates? This is the lunacy of the Fed and just watch, they will find out they have raised too fast and begin more QE and lower rates once again as the economy deflates. It's coming. The question is, when? It is after the deflationary episode though, that gold will sky rocket.

Listen to what Harvard Professor of Public Policy and Professor of Economics, Ken Rogoff had to say at the World Economic Forum (WEF) in Davos Switzerland at a panel called "The Next Financial Crisis."

"If we have another financial crisis, there isn't even a plan A," (He is referring to central bank options if one were to occur).

"When you see debt rising at an aggressive pace, you should definitely look out for that," he said. *"If something pushed up interest rates, if they went up in the places that had a lot of debt like Italy and Japan, some emerging markets, they could have a lot of problems."*

"It is not hard to imagine a stock price collapse -- it's built on price growth but also very low interest rates, and I don't know how everything from art to bitcoin will react."[5]

Please re-read what this economics professor said again and think about all you have read in this book. What more words than that do you need to hedge your portfolio with a little gold?

To put it in baseball terms, the damage the Fed has done to the monetary system can only be cured with a diversification into gold because there is no baseball commissioner (higher power) to force them to stop using the drug (stimulus). There's only you to figure things out on your own and protect your portfolio.

Any future QE stimulus by the Fed this time won't stop the deflationary contraction. It simply won't be enough. Those glory days you have had since 2009 will be over for possibly a good long time.

Now I think I'm going down to the well tonight
and I'm going to drink till I get my fill
And I hope when I get old I don't sit around thinking about it
but I probably will
Yeah, just sitting back trying to recapture
a little of the glory of, well time slips away
and leaves you with nothing mister but
boring stories of glory days
—Bruce Springsteen, *Glory Days*

Gold and the U.S. Dollar Index

Earlier we discussed the Dollar Index, which is what most people perceive to be the value of the dollar. What that Dollar Index represents however is the Euro at 57.6%, Japan/Yen 13.6%, UK/Pound 11.9%, Canada/Dollar 9.1%, Sweden/Krona 4.2%, and the Switzerland/Franc 3.6%. Those are the currencies that make up the Dollar Index or anytime you hear financial media say the dollar up or dollar down.

---

[5] https://www.cnbc.com/2018/01/23/rogoff-banks-dont-even-have-a-plan-a-for-another-financial-crisis.html

When you watch CNBC you never see the value of the dollar as an indicator to watch. You may see the Euro/Dollar or Yen/Dollar, but that's about it. **The Dollar Index is the basis of all your investments but if you ask anyone on Wall St. what a dollar is, they won't answer that it is a representation of all these other currencies.**

It's important you know how the dollar is doing because if the dollar falls, guess what? So, does the purchasing power of all your investments that are U.S. dollar based. If prices stayed the same on all your investments, you may think you are treading water. But if the dollar fell 10% during that time, guess what? Your investments will have 10% less purchasing power. This is inflation. And in 5 years your Federal Reserve wants to decrease your purchasing power 10% with their 2% inflation goal. Without the equivalent 2% gain in wages, your wealth will be depreciating. And if you are retired, you'll be losing money because that "risk free" asset the dollar isn't shooting off enough interest to compensate for the inflation.

Does comparing the value of the U.S. Dollar Index versus other depreciating currencies of the world give you the true value of the dollar? Of course, it doesn't. But valuing the U.S. dollar to the price of gold does give you a dose of reality.

One currency you can't really compare to gold is what Zimbabwe used to use as money. The next picture shows the result of Zimbabwe's currency inflation. It is the $100-trillion-dollar bill which was currency at one point. The purchasing power of the $100-trillion bill might have gotten you a loaf of bread in Zimbabwe when they first came out, but they became worthless too. Eventually though, they started showing up on eBay and have been selling for over $100 U.S. dollars and I imagine will keep appreciating. Maybe Zimbabweans should have considered this as a currency strategy!

Dow/Gold Ratio

The Dow/Gold ratio is another tool to know when stocks are of value and when gold is of value. To get this ratio, divide the Dow by the price of gold. Right now, that ratio is 19.62. As you can see from the following chart, it's just above where it was in 2008 when the stock market began to crash.

In 1929-1933 the Dow/Gold ratio fell to 2:1 and 2006-2011 got down to just over 6:1. These ratios tell you whether one or the other is of value or which one is a better buy. It's clear what that answer is.

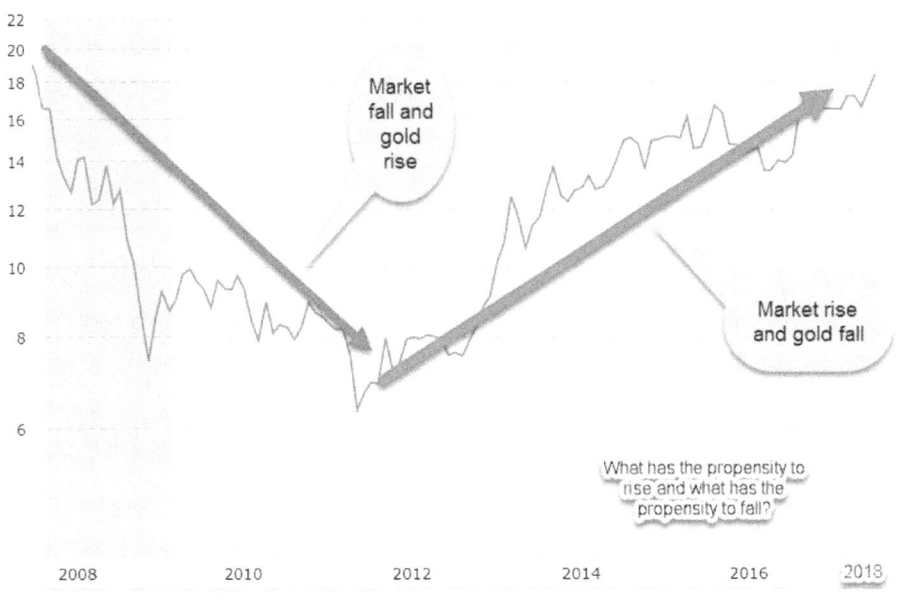

How Much of an Investors Assets Should Be Allocated to Gold?

A $5,000 or $10,000 investment in gold will buy you a nice vacation with the proceeds at some point in the future, but it won't protect your portfolio. You need to treat gold as a portfolio component to match your U.S. dollar exposure. When you insure your home from threat of fire, you don't insure just the kitchen and the family room, you insure the whole house.

Likewise, you need to insure your entire portfolio against the potential of a U.S. dollar decline. This may mean an allocation of 10% to 20%, depending on how much U.S. dollar exposure your portfolio has.

A conservative investor will only invest in physical gold and silver that you can touch. This means taking delivery of it or storing it somewhere that you can take delivery if necessary. Chapter 9 will explain what types of physical gold should be bought, and Part II will tell you what physical silver to acquire.

A moderate investor would put 10% investment into physical gold and silver as described in the coming chapters, along with an additional 10% investment into gold- and silver-mining stocks and the ETF (GDX).

An aggressive investor would put no more than 30% into gold and silver. Ten percent still needs to be put into physical gold and silver. Fifteen percent can be invested in the gold-mining stocks that represent the HUI Index or the ETF (GDX) and 5% in junior mining stocks or the ETF (GDXJ). More of these alternative gold investments available to moderate and aggressive investors are explained in Chapter 7.

What Assets to Sell to Put Into Gold?

If all your liquid assets are tied up in CDs, Treasuries, muni-bonds/funds, government securities/funds and money market accounts and you are a conservative investor, then you need the hedge gold provides since all of these investments are subject to the whims of a U.S. dollar decline.

When interest rates start to rise, bonds will fall. At some point in the future you'll want to sell some of those bond fund and other bond funds that have longer maturities to buy gold or silver. More and more cities will declare bankruptcy as the economy deteriorates and muni-bonds won't provide the security they once did.

Bond mutual funds would get hit too. The adage of "interest rates up, bond values down" holds true, and this means you will lose your principal when this occurs. Junk bonds especially so as more and more companies struggle with the credit contraction. Many investors will be hurt if they don't pay attention to this and actively manage their portfolios. Don't just wait to read your investment statement to get the bad news you're losing money. Be proactive with your investing. Do your homework on what rates are doing.

Keep in mind, interest rates may stay low for the time being while this deflationary episode plays itself out. Japan has had a few decades of low rates during their deflation, hovering around a 0% return. Rates could even go negative if the Fed wanted to get extreme. For now, bonds like treasuries are going to be at the bottom of Exter's Pyramid as a safe haven and at first will increase in value as the dollar gets stronger during the deflationary contraction (rush to safety or perceived safety).

Chapter 7
Types of Gold Investments

There are many ways to take advantage of a bull market in gold. This section explains the various types of vehicles in which one can invest, but only one, physical gold, is no one else's liability. I believe everyone should have some of the physical as a base for one's portfolio. That's not a biased gold dealer talking to you, but a person who understands and writes about our monetary system and the effects of Congressional and Federal Reserve policy on the purchasing power of your money. Always remember the difference between that 1964 quarter and the 1965 quarter. That explains everything why possessing physical metal is important.

The various ways to invest in gold that will be discussed are:

1. Physical Gold (Bullion Coins and Bars)
2. Exchange Traded Funds (ETFs) and Gold Mining ETFs
3. Stocks & Mutual Funds
4. Gold Certificates
5. Goldmoney Inc.
6. Leveraging Through Commodity Companies
7. Rare or Numismatic Coins

Physical Gold (Bullion Coins and Bars)

I recommend physical gold coins as the preferred way to invest in gold. In fact, I have dedicated an entire chapter to it (see Chapter 9).

This recommendation comes from the simple fact that physical gold is real wealth and all other paper forms of gold are geared more towards profit than insuring an investor's portfolio from U.S. dollar depreciation. In a sense, an investor gets the best of both worlds with physical gold. They can procure profit, but also guarantee themselves wealth if the current monetary system were to collapse.

Physical gold and silver are the only insurance one has against this possibility. I'm not saying the monetary system will collapse but having some gold and silver coins at home is "prudent."

Gold Bullion Coins

There are four different weights of gold bullion coins; 1/10-ounce, ¼-ounce, ½-ounce and 1-ounce. I'm only recommending people purchase one type of gold coin and that is the 1-ounce coin.

The reason to purchase the 1-ounce coin is that it has the smallest spread between the spot price of gold per ounce and the selling price of the coin (what you pay for it). The spot price of gold is what you see gold trading for on various websites. It changes minute by minute 24 hours a day, 5 days a week. The spread or premium is the difference between what a gold dealer pays to get the gold and what they charge you above that price paid.

As an example, for simplicity of understanding; If the spot price today is $1,000 per ounce of gold, the U.S. Mint will sell the gold to gold dealers at a 3% markup (premium) over spot.[1] The gold dealer would turn around and sell the gold to investors after taking his cut, anywhere from 2% to 10% over the premium. This means your final purchase price would be anywhere from 5% to 13% (spread or premium) over the spot price, depending on the gold dealer you purchase the gold and silver from. That's why it's important to ask questions of the dealer which we'll get into later in the book.

The premiums can change due to lack of supply or over supply, depending on what the price of gold is doing. There are times when certain coins may not be available at all because the U.S. Mint only produces so many coins a month and there must be a wait for production to keep up with demand. The U.S. Mint is mandated by law to keep pace with demand.

---

[1] The United States Mint - American Eagle Bullion Coins
http://usmint.gov/consumer/?flash=yes&action=americanEagles

The other reason for purchasing the 1-ounce gold bullion coin is because it is known the world over. Because of this recognition, it is easily exchangeable for the local currency which can be used for purchase of goods and services should it become necessary at some point in the future to do so.

With the 1/10-, ¼- and ½-ounce coins you are going to pay a spread that is well in excess of the 1-ounce coin, even as high as 30% with some dealers and that's why I don't like them. Some say you can sue the smaller gold coins for barter, but silver coins you'll see in the silver section work better for this.

The types of 1-ounce gold bullion coins I recommend are:

1. American Gold Eagle
2. American Gold Buffalo
3. Canadian Maple Leaf
4. South African Krugerrand
5. Chinese Gold Panda
6. Australian Kangaroo Nuggets

There are others, but these are the 1-ounce gold coins I would feel comfortable owning, as they all have the weight written on them in English. It will be easier to transact with a coin here in the U.S. if the weight is in ounces versus in kilograms.

American Eagle Gold Bullion Coin

The Gold Bullion Coin Act of 1985 authorized the first gold coins to be minted since the confiscation of gold in 1933.[2] These coins were named American Eagle and contain one ounce of gold. The remainder of the coin consists of 3% silver and 5.33% copper to keep the coin from losing gold content due to scratching or marring.

---

[2] Gold Bullion Coin Act of 1985
http://www.izagg.com/WealthBuilding/Postings/goldinfo3.htm

The obverse design features a rendition of Augustus Saint-Gaudens' full-length figure of Lady Liberty with flowing hair, holding a torch in her right hand and an olive branch in her left, with the Capitol building in the left background. The reverse design, by sculptor Miley Busiek, features a male eagle carrying an olive branch, flying above a nest containing a female eagle and her hatchlings.[3]

The American Gold Buffalo is a 24-karat pure gold coin and is the first such coin minted by the U.S. Mint. The 24-karat pure gold coins are harder to counterfeit as they are .9999% gold. So far there haven't been any reports of counterfeiting in the U.S.

The Buffalo is based upon American sculptor James Earle Fraser's revered Buffalo Nickel of 1913. It displays Fraser's classic design of an American Indian on the coin's obverse and the American bison on the reverse.[4]

---

[3] Wiki – American Eagle Gold Coin
http://en.wikipedia.org/wiki/American_Gold_Eagle
[4] Wiki – American Buffalo Gold Coin
http://en.wikipedia.org/wiki/American_Buffalo_%28coin%29

Gold Bars

Gold bars are my favorite of all gold investments because they are simply a way to acquire gold closer to the spot price. The more you buy, the lower the cost per ounce is. They are just as liquid with gold dealers as coins are, but not as popular only because many trust the American Gold Eagle U.S. Mint produced coins

There are gold bars that weigh anywhere from one ounce to 400 ounces and are catching on in popularity. The 100 and 400-ounce bars are primarily utilized in the COMEX market and most traders never take delivery. They just trade for profit or for clients like large banks, financial institutions and Central Banks.

There are many different companies that manufacture gold bars. The more well-known ones for the 1-ounce bars traded in the U.S. are Royal Canadian Mint (RCM), Sunshine Mint, Credit Suisse (bars manufactured by Valcambi), Produits Artistiques de M'taux Pr'cieux (PAMP) and Republic Metals Corporation (RMC). These bars are 24-karat, .9999% fine gold and thus more difficult to counterfeit. Most of these gold bars are easily traded throughout the world and will follow the price of gold up and down just as coins do. Gold bars are also now even appearing in vending machines in some countries. See picture of Credit Suisse and PAMP gold bars.

Many people just assume the gold dealer will buy back the gold. Even reputable gold dealers may not buy your gold bars back from you, while others will require you to get them assayed first.

The main reason to store your gold bars at the place you bought them, however, is that you can sell them at a moment's notice with just a phone call, while still maintaining the ability to take delivery at any time.

Exchange Traded Funds (ETFs)[5]

ETFs offer ways for investors to invest in physical gold or a basket of gold-mining stocks. They are primarily used by investors as a low-cost way to play the gold market.

Physical Gold ETFs

In the U.S., the four most popular gold ETF's are; the streetTRACKS Gold Trust (GLD), the Ishares Comex Gold Trust (IAU), VanEck Merk Gold Trust (OUNZ), and the Sprott Physical Gold Trust (PHYS). [6,7,8]

---

[5] Exchange Traded Funds U.S. Securities and Exchange Commission http://www.sec.gov/answers/etf.htm
[6] SPDR Gold Shares Symbol: GLD http://www.spdrgoldshares.com/#usa

These ETFs offer investors a way to play the gold market, but do not allow the investor to take delivery of the gold unless you have large accounts and pay high fees to acquire. Your average investor just wouldn't need to do that, and these ETFs should be for traders only, not long-term holders of gold because of the fees involved you have to pay each year.

The gold is set aside in a bank depository. One can buy shares in the ETF and sell the shares back when they liquidate their position.

These ETFs are a lower-cost way to invest in gold but are only paper promises if the dollar were to collapse, as the investor does not have actual ownership of gold whereby they can take delivery by turning in their shares if investing smaller amounts typically under $100,000 (some offer lower amounts but the fees to liquidate are exorbitant – check with the prospectus before investing).

A bank is typically used to be the custodian of your gold and personally, I don't want a bank to be in control of my gold. I want to be in control of my wealth.

Something else to think about when it comes to the supply issue during a real push higher on the price of gold is, where will these ETFs get their gold? When the price of gold moves from its current second stage to its third stage of euphoria, it will be impossible for these ETFs to find the gold needed to deposit for each investor who wants shares. There are other issues that one must consider, that relate to whether the ETF who has all that gold is at the same time leasing it out.

Big money hedge funds and mutual funds will be fighting with the little guy in trying to take advantage of this gold bull run, especially as the economy deteriorates. These ETFs could be forced to freeze all assets if there is a problem with the custodian.

Here is what the ETF: GLD prospectus says in such a case:

> "In the case of the insolvency of the Custodian, a liquidator may seek to freeze access to the gold held in all of the accounts held by the Custodian,

---

[7] iShares COMEX Gold Symbol: IAU
http://us.ishares.com/product_info/fund/overview/IAU.htm

[8] http://www.merkgold.com/overview.html http://sprottphysicalbullion.com

including the Trust Allocated Account. Although the Trust would be able to claim ownership of properly allocated gold bars, the Trust could incur expenses in connection with asserting such claims, and the assertion of such a claim by the liquidator could delay creations and redemptions of Baskets. In issuing Baskets, the Trustee relies on certain information received from the Custodian which is subject to confirmation after the Trustee has relied on the information. If such information turns out to be incorrect, Baskets may be issued in exchange for an amount of gold which is more or less than the amount of gold which is required to be deposited with the Trust."[9]

One other issue with the gold ETF's described in the prospectus is that if the bank were to be robbed, the gold set aside for you is not covered for theft… and it's your loss. This may be a far-fetched thought but is not out of the realm of possibility. Add to this scenario that the gold may not be insured. It's all in the prospectus that one must read before considering this type of investment. Most don't do their due diligence, as they just trust the word of their financial advisor. After all, they're the experts.

From the ETF: GLD prospectus:[10]

"The Trust may not have adequate sources of recovery if its gold is lost, damaged, stolen or destroyed and recovery may be limited, even in the event of fraud, to the market value of the gold at the time the fraud is discovered. The Trust does not insure its gold."

Wouldn't it be better to secure your own gold and keep an eye on it yourself? At least you could obtain insurance on your hoard or read the storage section later in this book for ideas on what to do.

ETF mutual funds and mining stocks will be the only products your financial advisor wants to sell to you, because there is no profit in selling you physical gold, or they don't even have the ability to sell

---

[9] GLD Prospectus
http://www.spdrgoldshares.com/media/GLD/file/SPDRGoldTrustProspectus.pdf
[10] Ibid

physical gold (and silver). More than likely they will push the paper gold and silver ETFs as being the equivalent to gold. They are not.

Gold Mining ETFs

There are gold mining companies that one can invest in, but it's not the same as investing in physical gold. The risk is more although if your timing is good, the reward can be good as well.

GDX is the symbol for the Gold Miners ETF.[11] It seeks to replicate the performance of the AMEX Gold Miners index.[12]

GDXJ is the symbol for the Junior Gold Miners ETF and seeks to replicate the price and yield performance of the Market Vectors Junior Gold Miners Index.[13,14]

ETFs are becoming more and more popular compared to mutual funds because of the ease of getting in and out during the market rather than waiting for the order to be filled at the end of the day. The fees and commissions generally tend to be lower compared to most mutual funds.

Stocks and Mutual Funds

Investing in gold-mining stocks or gold funds is not the same as investing in physical gold itself. Besides being a paper ownership that is non-convertible to the physical metal, there are issues like cost of mining the gold, cash flow problems, debt-to-equity ratios, management problems, political factors with foreign ownership like companies in Africa, Venezuela, Ecuador and Russia among others, and how much gold might be in the mines themselves. Investing in

---

[11] GDX – Gold Miners ETF Prospectus
http://www.vaneck.com/sld/vaneck//offerings/factsheets/GDX_FactSheet.pdf
[12] NYSE Arca Gold Miners
http://www.amex.com/othProd/prodInf/OpPiIndComp.jsp?Product_Symbol=GDM
[13] GDXJ – Junior Gold Miners ETF http://www.vaneck.com/funds/GDXJ.aspx
[14] Market Vectors Junior Gold Miners Index - Ibid

physical gold directly takes all the guesswork out of the equation, which is why physical gold is a more conservative way to go.

Moderate and aggressive investors can do well in these mutual fund vehicles, and they also can lose big, as many did in 2008 when gold crashed. These investments can be purchased through a dollar-cost averaging approach on any big dips in the price of gold.

If a company has known gold holdings and mines full of gold to unearth, there is value based on the price of gold. This means the value of the company can go higher without doing anything except receiving the benefit of the higher price of the gold they already have mined going higher as well as what is their assumed gold still in the earth to be mined on the properties they own. However, in 2008 almost all gold-mining companies took a big hit, yet gold itself ended up positive for the year. Some of the Junior Mining companies lost 80% of their value during this decline. As with any investment, it's a timing thing and you must know where the price of gold is in its cycle, as well as what the chart says for your gold mining stock investment. The adage, buy low, sell high comes to mind.

Gold Mining Stocks (Blue Chip companies and Junior Mining companies)

Blue Chip

Two of the largest gold-mining stocks are Newmont Mining (NYSE: NEM) and Barrick Gold (NYSE: ABX).

Most gold stock investors will choose to invest in the gold-mining companies that make up the HUI index. These companies are "unhedged," meaning they do not short the gold market or hedge against any potential decline in the price of gold. In a gold bull market, it is better to stick with companies that do not hedge. Most companies, though, have ceased their hedging business with the run-up in the price of gold over the last 10 years.

The following are the 15 companies that make up the HUI Index, with their stock symbols and composition percentage:

Company name	Symbol	Weighting[nb 1]
Goldcorp Inc	NYSE: GG	16.59%
Barrick Gold Corp	NYSE: ABX	11.87%
Alamos Gold Inc	NYSE: AGI	9.49%
Newmont Mining Corp	NYSE: NEM	9.27%
AngloGold Ashanti Ltd	NYSE: AU	5.70%
Gold Fields Ltd	NYSE: GFI	5.66%
Randgold Resources Ltd	NASDAQ: GOLD	5.34%
Sibanye Gold Ltd	NYSE: SBGL	5.23%
New Gold Inc	AMEX: NGD	5.18%
Kinross Gold Corp	NYSE: KGC	5.06%
Agnico Eagle Mines Ltd	NYSE: AEM	4.91%
Eldorado Gold Corp	NYSE: EGO	4.81%
Cia de Minas Buenaventura SAA	NYSE: BVN	4.10%
Harmony Gold Mining Co Ltd	NYSE: HMY	3.40%
Yamana Gold Inc	NYSE: AUY	3.40%

Junior Mining Stocks

Gold-mining stocks known as "juniors" are companies that primarily explore for gold. They are typically cash-strapped and risky investments but may pay off big if gold is found through their mining operations. When gold is found, one of the larger companies may purchase the junior miner, and this is where the investor can be paid off handsomely.

The last thing you want to do is invest in a company that has no cash. The debt load of some of these companies could lead to collapse if enough time goes by without any kind of a gold discovery.

Unless someone does due diligence on these junior mining companies, the only way I recommend investing in this segment of the market, for aggressive investors only, is through the ETF: GDXJ mentioned earlier. It is best to do your homework before considering these companies, and no more than 5% of an aggressive investor's portfolio should be allocated to the juniors.

Top 25 Holdings	% Portfolio Weight
Gold Fields Ltd ADR	4.12
Pan American Silver Corp	3.89
Iamgold Corp	3.80
Sibanye-Stillwater ADR	3.80
Kirkland Lake Gold Ltd	3.77
Yamana Gold Inc	3.71
New Gold Inc	3.54
Evolution Mining Ltd	3.49
Northern Star Resources Ltd	3.32
B2Gold Corp	3.10
Centamin PLC	2.95
Pretium Resources Inc	2.77
Detour Gold Corp	2.67
OceanaGold Corp	2.63
Hecla Mining Co	2.56
Regis Resources Ltd	2.47
Alamos Gold Inc	2.15
Osisko Gold Royalties Ltd	2.11
Tahoe Resources Inc	2.08
SSR Mining Inc	1.97
First Majestic Silver Corp	1.91
Coeur Mining Inc	1.86
Endeavour Mining Corp	1.82
Centerra Gold Inc	1.80
St Barbara Ltd	1.62

Gold-Oriented Funds (Mutual Funds, Closed-End Funds)

If one doesn't have the time to decipher which of the multitude of gold-mining stocks to invest in, they may turn to a professional manager to do the investing for them by investing via a mutual fund or closed-end fund like CEF. Managers of mutual funds buy and sell individual mining stocks based on what they think this sector of the market will do.

A closed-end fund like CEF invests in physical gold and is a viable option for those inclined, but it's still paper gold of which you can't take delivery.[15]

The one thing you'll find common with many gold-mining stock mutual funds are the higher fees. A couple of gold mutual funds are First Gold Eagle fund, symbol SGGDX: $2.3 billion in assets, 5 stars from Morningstar, holds 17.88% in physical gold in 2010, but with the fall in the price of gold, the net assets has fallen to 1.23 billion by 2018 with total physical gold holdings of 18.06%. ; and Tocqueville Gold fund, symbol TGLDX: $1.4 billion in assets, 4 stars from Morningstar, holds 9.48% in physical gold in 2010 and by 2018, 1.21 billion and 12.36% in gold bars. You can see that as the price of gold falls, these funds allocate more to physical gold than to the mining stocks.[16,17]

Gold Certificates

Gold certificates offer an intriguing way to own gold. While this type of option does incur storage fees that take profit away from your investment, there are options for taking delivery. There is only one gold certificate worth looking at, since it is backed by the Australian

---

[15] CEF http://www.centralfund.com/
[16] First Eagle Gold A | SGGDX First Eagle Gold
http://quote.morningstar.com/fund/f.aspx?t=SGGDX
[17] Tocqueville Gold | TGLDX Tocqueville Gold
http://quote.morningstar.com/fund/f.aspx?t=TGLDX

government. This certificate is sold by the Perth Mint and is a way to keep funds offshore.

Ownership of Perth Mint certificates by no means excuses you from reporting gains to the IRS. Failing to declare to the IRS any taxes owed upon closing the account is an invitation at some point to an audit, and subsequent fines and/or jail time if the IRS gets wind of your transactions.

The IRS will always find a way of finding your assets, just as they tried to do in getting the Swiss bank UBS to disclose who their American clients were and how much they had hidden at their bank. The penalties of not disclosing to the IRS any offshore holdings are too severe to not report ownership.

Perth Mint

The Perth Mint is owned by the Western Australian government, which took over from the British in 1970. It is a well-established company in existence for over 100 years. Today the Perth Mint "facilitates investment in precious metals not only by supplying coins and bars, but by also providing the opportunity for investing in precious metals without the issues associated with taking physical metal, through the various products offered through Perth Mint Depository. One of these is the Perth Mint Gold product quoted on the Australian Stock Exchange."[18]

In a sense, the Federal Reserve Note at one time was a gold certificate, as the holder of that note could redeem it for gold. At least they could up until 1933, when the government confiscated gold. Confiscation is discussed in detail in Chapter 8.

---

[18] Perth Mint Certificates, Australia
http://www.perthmint.com.au/about_us_the_perth_mint.aspx

Goldmoney Inc. (TSX:XAU)

Goldmoney is a way to buy and sell gold and hold in other countries. It is also a way to transact in gold. There is also an option they have for trading/storing cryptocurrencies like Bitcoin. I get into the detail and relevancy of cryptocurrencies in the 2018 revised version of my Illusions of Wealth book.

From the Goldmoney website they say you can do the following with Goldmoney; Buy, sell, and hold physical gold, silver, platinum, and palladium bullion online. Fully-reserved accounts with audited (one-to-one) metal ownership. Insured accounts Insured custody and storage at multiple vaults around the world. Spend or withdraw cash directly from your Holding with the Goldmoney Prepaid card. Redeem gold Redeem bullion bars and coins at vaults and Goldmoney branches or have them shipped to your home. Comprehensive reporting, low cost dealing and storage fees, and multiple funding options including bank transfer, debit and credit cards, and cryptocurrencies. Hold nine currencies Hold in reserve or exchange up to nine currencies (USD, GBP, EUR, CAD, CHF, JPY NZD, HKD, AUD) without paying foreign exchange fees. Free metal and currency payments to other Goldmoney Holdings. Recurring savings plans and retirement accounts. Mobile app for iPhone and Android. Trusted customer service – your personal Relationship Manager is available via phone, email, and secure messaging directly from your Holding Dashboard. Holdings can be owned by individuals, joint owners, corporations, and trusts.

As far as crypto trading goes, the fact that this is a listed company gives one a little peace of mind in trading cryptocurrencies versus some of the other exchanges in existence. The fact that the CME allows some cryptocurrencies to be traded in futures gives these coins more legitimacy. I go into more depth of cryptocurrencies in the 2018 updated version of Illusions of Wealth.

Leveraging Through Commodity Companies

Monex

Another way to invest in gold and silver is through Monex Deposit Company.[19] The fees charged by Monex are reasonable versus a gold dealer, yet their salespeople make their money convincing investors to leverage their investment at a 3-1 to 5-1 ratio, which has given them a bad rap. Needless to say, there is much risk in doing this.

Leveraging means an investor will take a sum of money, say $10,000 and be able to buy up to 3 to 5 times that amount, or up to $50,000 worth of gold, by borrowing $40,000 and paying interest on the loan. The selling of these products stems from the fact that brokers with Monex are compensated at a higher rate than just selling bullion gold and silver metal and thus will try and obtain higher compensation through selling the leveraged products.

If gold fell by 10%, they would actually be down 10% of $50,000, or $5,000. The original $10,000 investment has become $5,000, and a further decline in the price of gold could trigger a margin call.

When investors lose money this way, they aren't happy. Because gold investments are sold to investors, they may not know what they were getting into to begin with. It seems this is true with Monex, as they had an "F" rating from the Better Business Bureau (BBB) at one point in time but somehow were able to get rid of that and come back with a BBB No Rating status.[20]

The U.S. Commodity Futures Trading Commission (CFTC) filed a civil lawsuit against Monex for $290 million in September of 2017. They are calling it the "biggest-ever retail precious metals fraud enforcement action brought by the regulator." I warned about Monex in the 2010 version of this book.[21]

---

[19] Monex Precious Metals http://www.monex.com/about/index.html
[20] Monex BBB Rating http://www.la.bbb.org/Business-Report/Monex-24970
[21] https://www.reuters.com/article/us-cftc-enforcement/cftc-sues-california-gold-

Because of this leverage risk, I don't recommend this trade at all for conservative and moderate investors. Greed is something my father, a retired commodities broker, always said is the main reason people lose money. Aggressive investors who know what they are doing could profit from this type of investment, but no more than 5% should be allocated to it. Just watch out for the greed, as leverage is a risky venture. Be conservative if using leverage. Go for small victories and sell and keep tight stops if you are wrong.

Rare, Semi-rate and Numismatic Coins

Rare coins are typically coins that have been graded by recognized grading services PCGS (Professional Coin Grading Service) or NGC (National Guaranty Association).

A grade of "70" by one of these companies would be considered a flawless coin and would command the highest price in that category. If coins do not meet the minimum requirement to be given a grade, they can still be considered "rare" and sold at a premium because of the age of the coin.

Rare coins peaked in 1989 and fell in value 85% by 2001 and haven't recovered since. Some may be recovering because of the actual silver or gold content in the coin. Yet to listen to the salespeople who work for the companies that advertise on TV and radio, one would think that these coins were going to go to the moon again if the economy were to decline. Perhaps this euphoria they represent is centered around the fact that many of these salespeople who work for gold dealers that do the advertising make 15% to 30% and more in commissions on these sales.

After paying those kinds of commission, you must earn even more than that just to break even. The fact that the gold content will increase

---

dealer-monex-in-fraud-scheme-idUSKCN1BH2HA

the value of the coin is the only real appreciation you can expect on your investment in these coins.

I have devoted the entire next chapter to the tricks that salespeople of rare coins will utilize to get people to invest. The problem is, gold dealers are not regulated by anyone and are high on promise and low on delivery of profit. It is not that these gold dealers need to be regulated by government, the SEC or the CFTC, but that individuals need to be educated as to their tactics in selling high-priced rare coins. This is why I devote more to this subject… to educate the gold and silver buyer.

Gold dealers will use every trick in the book to get potential investors to forget about investing in gold bullion and end up selling them either a shiny coin or something else that won't be easily liquidated if the U.S. dollar were to decline, except for the gold or silver content value of the coin. Most buyers of rare coins won't realize they got ripped off until it comes time to liquidate one's collection or the children as recipients of the coins after their parents pass away. I know as I have received phone calls from those children who inherited the coins.

What investors need to do is buy bullion gold with their ever-decreasing Federal Reserve Notes today, to hedge their U.S. dollar-based portfolio and possess some real wealth so they can still go buy food, medicine and make ends meet in the future.

I may buy a few rare coins because they are aesthetically beautiful, but not as an investment.

Chapter 8

Who Is Recommending Gold and Why?

When it comes to investing in gold, most people first hear about it not from their financial advisor, but from a radio or TV advertisement. We know most financial advisors don't recommend an allocation to gold, so if an investor is to hear about it, it's probably from one of those scary TV commercials that claim the dollar is going to crash and financial Armageddon is around the corner and you need to buy gold now!

The number of companies that advertise on the radio and TV is growing. I'm aware of advertisements for various gold dealers over the past few years on the radio and/or TV shows of Sean Hannity, Glenn Beck, Rush Limbaugh, Michael Medved, Laura Ingraham, Dennis Prager, George Noory and Neil Boortz on the right, and Randi Rhodes, Ed Schultz and Stephanie Miller on the left.[1]

Gold dealers mostly advertise on right-wing radio and television shows. That's because most of the buyers of gold are conservatives based on marketing analysis that shows this to be the case. In reality, politics don't matter to the gold dealers' salespeople as long as they have a live person calling in they can influence to buy gold. These gold dealers even hire the main radio personality, like they have in the past with Sean Hannity, Glenn Beck, Mark Levin and Neil Boortz, touting the gold company.

If the person who calls in says they want to buy gold, nine out of 10 have no clue at all about buying gold. Our education system teaches us nothing about it as I have pointed out. I know this personally to be the case because I worked for one of the nation's largest gold dealers, Goldline International, for six months in 2006 and took hundreds of calls a week from the public and speaking with the marketing director there to see where the leads mostly came from.

---

[1] These are ads that author has either been seen or heard personally by the author.

I tried as much as I could to give big discounts for coins they wanted me to sell as the price of gold that time was under $500 an ounce and silver around $5 an ounce. Anyone I sold to at that time has doubled their value or more because of the price of gold and silver moving higher. Gold subsequently went to a high of over $1,920 and silver to $49.50 by 2011 and of course have since retreated before they take off higher again as discussed.

Since I discovered how the industry worked, and more importantly how gold dealers work, I decided to educate people how to buy gold and silver at the lowest cost to spot and wrote the first version of this book and started my own company to sell precious metals but do it in a way at the lowest cost. Now I'm writing a second version as gold dealers tactics keep changing and you the buyer need to be aware of the new ways they try and rip you off.

Gold dealers simply frown when their sales people sell just gold or silver bullion because there are no big profits in them for their owners. Any agent who just sells bullion would be fired for lack of production. I know an agent from one company that told me if he or his associates weren't booking over $100,000 in commissions, that they would be out the door. That's your money they are taking from you.

If you're reading this book now and are educated about the choices before you buy gold or silver, you made a good decision that can save you thousands in commissions. This book is written to show you the best way to insure your portfolio from the fall of the U.S. dollar with the right type of gold and silver in your portfolio. The only gold and silver you need to accomplish this are bullion coins and bars. I will go into more detail with recommendations in Chapter 9.

I'm writing this section of the book to warn people as to the lengths gold dealers will go to and the tactics they will utilize in selling high commissioned products to unsuspecting buyers. Who better to expose their tactics than someone who was an insider? I even was solicited by the Santa Monica City Attorney and my testimony was instrumental in getting a $6 million settlement against one gold dealer for investors who were taken advantage of. Of course, the gold dealer admitted they did no wrong in the settlement and $6 million to them when their sales of gold is in the high millions doesn't do them much harm.

I could run the same type of gold dealer business and make more money doing it, but I would rather be the low-cost company and say what I know or think about metals in my articles without pushing investors to high commissioned products and **feel good about what I do.** In fact, there is not one of these gold dealers that sells rare, semi-rare, European and numismatic coins out there who has a main person or owner that has written a book on buying gold. I've written two on investing and am proud of how I can bring awareness to investors. The problem is, most investors don't do their homework when it comes to gold.

The Dirt on Gold Dealers' Tactics

People who work for gold dealers do not need any licenses to sell gold, or specific investment training to get hired. I was hired because they liked that I had over 20 years' experience as a financial advisor but my real goal was to get to know the industry that the financial services industry ignored, and then offer the products to the public that these other gold dealers hate to sell because they are in the investors best interest.

You have to be careful because these charlatan's or snake oil salesmen have been doing this a long time and they have got rich off of those who invested with them and unfortunately many investors don't even know they have got ripped off.

What happens when the gold dealer's salesperson answers the phone and greets you for the first time?

The gold salesman will immediately try and build the relationship, like all good salespeople do. They will try and see what your hot buttons are, whether it is the frail economy, inept Congress, potential stock market decline, crashing dollar or whatever the hot topic of the day may be like war with North Korea or ISIS or other Middle East issues. It's not too difficult to find someone's hot button.

These sales people are trained to utilize whatever information the caller gives them and will ask direct questions about their financial situation. Most people will comply and tell them about their various accounts. Why? Because they heard the advertisement on Glenn Beck's or Mark Levin's radio show, so these people must be trustworthy referrers, right?

The salesperson will say all the right things, like "help protect your purchasing power from inflation and a falling dollar," "gold is selling at a discount and you must act now before the price goes up." The salespeople already have an idea of what they are going to sell you, and no matter what your answer is to their questions, the conversation is always going to be directed to what the gold salesperson wants to sell, not which product fits the objectives of the buyer.

Some of the coins that gold dealers want to sell people are Swiss francs, French francs and others, known in the industry as *European* coins. These are older bullion coins from Europe and are sold with a premium of 15% to 30% or more over the spot price of gold. These European coins are sometimes referred to being semi-rare, but they are not. They are also not very liquid.

Many people pay thousands to tens of thousands of dollars extra for these coins, not knowing what they are really buying. When these folks call into the company to ask how their gold investment is performing, the gold salesman will give them the current price people buy the coins for, not the actual buy-back price. And here is the question that you need to write down and ask all gold dealers you contact to purchase gold and silver from <u>after</u> they have told you what they recommend and the cost for them;

"If I buy these coins from you for $x amount that you quoted me, at the current spot price, what will you buy these coins back from me for today with that same spot price?" The answer will not be straight forward as it should be. If it's not, the gold dealer is ripping you off. The truth is, the buyback price will more than likely be 20% to 30%

below your actual cost and you'll have to earn 30% to 40% just to break even on the investment.

Here's an example of how a sales pitch for the European coins like the Swiss francs would go:

Gold Salesperson:

> "Another kind of gold that has some additional benefits is the Swiss 20-franc coin. With these, you get the price appreciation and the hedge against inflation, but you also get the protection from government confiscation. So for a few dollars more, you get gold that can't be taken away from you.
>
> The government cannot confiscate any type of gold that has a collectible value.
>
> With the Swiss francs, you also have gold that is non-reportable. We don't generate any 1099s and don't ask for your Social Security number."

There are a few misleading statements in this sales pitch related to confiscation and the insinuation that the sale of gold coins is "non-reportable." Yes, they are non-reportable by the gold dealer today, but the sale needs to be reported by the investor to the IRS if there are any gains when sold.

I've given the confiscation issue its own section, which follows. The gold dealer who used confiscation in their sales tactics that had to pay $6 million in restitution to their investors was told by the Santa Monica City Attorney that they couldn't use the words "confiscation" in their sale approach or literature any longer. But there are still companies out there that will do this, so beware of them.

Gold Dealer Sales Tactics

Confiscation

The confiscation story, which is hard for most to overcome, is rather convincing. But after reading the following, the investor will possess the power to just say no to their confiscation ploy.

Gold salespeople will say things like, "Are you aware that in 1933, the government took gold coins away?" Most people don't realize this is true.

The gold salesperson will then ask, "What kind of gold do you want, the gold that can be confiscated, or the gold that can't?" Or word the question this way: "Do you want government gold or private gold?" "Government gold" would be the bullion gold like American Eagle gold bullion coins and bars and "private gold" would be the coins like the European coins or others with a high markup over the spot price of gold (these latter ones are all the gold sales person wants to sell as it pays them the most commission).

Many gold salesmen will try and convince you that if you buy gold bullion coins, the government will confiscate them like they did in 1933 with an executive order. They'll say that pre-1933 coins didn't get confiscated and if you buy these pre-1933 coins, the government won't confiscate them from you today. This is pure speculation on behalf of the gold salesperson. Yes, gold was confiscated in 1933. However, those laws and executive orders are no longer valid. They have all been rescinded. Don't let gold dealers convince you otherwise.

The following explains the facts of the gold confiscation. The only people who will probably read this in detail are gold salespeople, who won't be too happy about their hand being exposed. Quite a bit of their profit comes from this one tactic alone.

Executive Order 6102 was signed by President Roosevelt on April 5, 1933, "forbidding the Hoarding of Gold Coin, Gold Bullion and Gold Certificates."

Executive Order 6260, August 28, 1933 amended 6102 by saying:

> "...no returns (of gold to the government) are required to be filed with respect to Gold coin having a recognized special value to collectors of rare and unusual coin;"

Gold salespeople will say there was an amendment to this executive order on December 28, 1933 "Exempting Pre-1933 Gold Coins from Confiscation." No such executive order amendment from that date exists, although there were other amendments to Executive Order 6260.

Finally, Executive Order No. 11825, written December 31st, 1974, revoked Executive Orders 6102 and 6260.

So, what does this mean? It means no executive order exists today to confiscate anyone's gold.

Many gold dealers will say the following is of significance regarding which coins are considered "collectible" and thus would be exempt from confiscation:

> Title 31 of Code of Federal Regulations Sec. 54.20 Rare Coin:
>
> (b) Gold coin made prior to April 5, 1933, is considered to be of recognized special value to collectors of rare and unusual coin.

While it is true that these coins may be collectors' coins, it is irrelevant because again, all executive orders pertaining to confiscation of gold have been rescinded.

First Strike or Early Release Scam

Another ploy gold dealers utilize is to get people to buy their bullion coins that normally have a 2% to 10% markup at a 30% to 100% markup. What they do is get the new American Eagle coins produced at the U.S. Mint that come out of production early each year in January, certified by NGC as a higher value collector's coin that may someday be worth much more.

They may call these coins "First Strike" and have their salespeople tell prospective buyers that these coins were the first minted for a certain year (the first 100,000, let's say) and therefore are more valuable than the coins minted later in the year.

What the gold dealer will do is buy the American Eagle gold or silver bullion coins from the U.S. Mint for the normal 3% or so markup in price over spot. They will take this coin and send it to NGC and have it graded. The cost to grade the coins is minimal.

The coins will come back graded an MS 69 on average, with some coming back as a MS 70. Now the gold dealer can sell these coins with a 100% or more mark up over the spot price of gold. This is pure genius from the perspective of the gold dealer, if you ask me. Take a product worth x and sell it for 2x through the telling of a fable.

However, since there was no way to prove the coins were "First Strike" coins, NGC and the gold dealers had to regroup and subsequently came up with the new description "Early Releases," which they use today.[2]

From the NGC site:[3]

> To qualify for Early Releases designation, all coins must be received by NGC within 30 days of their release by the US Mint, or documented as being received by an NGC approved depository within this same 30-day period. Coins being sent directly to NGC do not need to be accompanied by original packaging or shipped in sealed mint boxes, but must arrive within the time period described above. The Early Releases request must be noted on the submission invoice, and additional service fees apply for the special label and designation verification.

The ability of gold dealers to profit on such a story is in my opinion one of the reasons the U.S. Mint keeps running out of coins at the beginning of the year sometimes. What gold dealer wouldn't want to double their money at the expense of the buyer? Not all gold dealers are alike, and if an investor is prepared with the right questions, they can separate the good ones from the bad ones. Caveat emptor!

---

[2] NGC Early Releases http://www.ngccoin.com/services/earlyrelease.asp
[3] Ibid

Doug Eberhardt

The Biggest Scam Going Now; 1.5 Ounce Silver Coins Touted by Gold Dealers

If you are buying 1.5-ounce Grizzly Bear, Polar Bear & Cub and other coins from Lear Captial, APMEX, JM Bullion, Penn Metals or other gold dealers you are blatantly getting ripped off. The graphic below is an example of the lowest cost of these coins from APMEX where if you buy these Polar Bear & Cub coins you will have to earn 30.00% just to break even. The same is true for the 1.5-ounce silver Snow Falcon, 1.5-ounce silver SuperLeaf, 1.5-ounce silver Polar Bear coins. Also, you'll rarely see on the website the buyback listed for these coins. It's much less than the purchase price. Some places that sell them won't even buy back the coins they sell.

Here's an example of how the coins are priced straight from the APMEX website for the 2015 Polar Bear & Cub 1.5-ounce silver coins. Notice the APMEX Buy Price and how much lower it is than the sell price. Other companies are much worse than this.

Buy Gold and Silver Safely

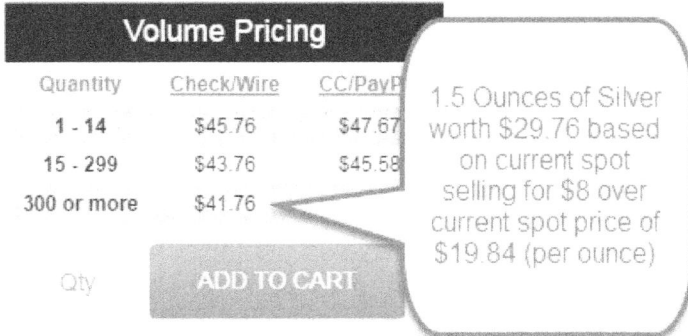

I had someone contact me whose father had passed away and they wanted to sell the 1.5-ounce coins. I called around to see who would take them and one company flat out told me they wouldn't buy them as they had too many in stock right now.

With bullion silver round coins, which you'll learn about in the silver section, you only must earn about 2.9% over spot to break even as of this writing. Big difference in profit in your pocket as the price of silver rises, not the gold dealer's pockets.

Buy Gold Bullion Coins and Leave the Rare Coins to the Speculators.

Another tactic gold dealers will use is if a caller is adamant about buying bullion coins like the American Eagle 1-ounce bullion coins, they will write up the order, but can't confirm the price until they receive a check or have the money wired in (the check of course would have to clear first). Once the gold dealer has the money in-house, they will call the buyer back and attempt to switch them to the rare collectors' coins. If that gold sales representative fails to do so, they will get one of the in-house seasoned pros on the line to hardball you, scare you, play upon all your fears about what's going on in the economy and how the government is going to someday take your gold from you, in trying one last effort to get the sale of the high commission coins. Their pressure is immense and if one is older (seniors), many succumb to it.

The senior sales representative gets on the phone to try and talk the buyer out of purchasing gold bullion coins and make them feel guilty about their purchase, even to the extent of yelling at them or calling them an idiot. Then they will put the buyer on hold for five minutes for no reason if they don't get their way. They will treat the bullion buyer like dirt, so the buyer needs to expect this treatment and keep asking "when will I receive my coins?" Even then, make sure the coins received are the coins ordered and for the price quoted by checking the paperwork.

One person who recently criticized the gold dealer industry and in particular Goldline International and its relationship with Glenn Beck, was former Representative Anthony Weiner (D-NY), well before he got into trouble as a predator.[4] Unfortunately Representative Weiner

---

[4] An Investigation of Goldline International by Representative Anthony Weiner http://weiner.house.gov/Reports/GoldlineReport.pdf

made the mistake of trying to make it a conservative-only issue rather than addressing the industry at large.

This critique by Weiner stems from the fact that Goldline had on its site at the time a "who's who" list of right wing personalities hawking gold for them, headline by Glenn Beck.[5] Goldline simply understands that their biggest clients are typically conservative.

What Weiner was upset with were the higher fees Goldline charges their clients to "rip them off." Goldline's rebuttal was that they disclose everything as to what their charges are. This is true, but it is how they disclose this information that slides by the typically ignorant buyer of gold.

When I worked at Goldline to learn about the industry for 6 months, before I decided to expose the industry and start my own company, the fees were not disclosed to a buyer at Goldline by the representative on the phone who does the selling, unless asked by the caller, but only disclosed in a rapid-fire manner by a separate person who does the confirmation of the trade. They may have changed this after getting sued, but I know Lear Capital does the same thing if you read about their tactics through Consumer Reports search on Google and their replies to customers.

After the confirmation, the sales rep gets back on the phone, thanks them for their purchase and the deal is done. If you go to try and sell a week later after buyer's remorse, you won't get a refund because you just agreed to getting ripped off on a recorded line.

After the recorded confirmation of the sale, the client is sent out a Risk Disclosure statement explaining the fees.

Here is Goldline's disclosure statement from 2006:[6]

> There is a price differential or "spread" between our selling price (the "ask" price) and our buy-back price (the "bid" price). This is often referred to as a "transaction cost." A typical spread on our most common bullion

---

[5] Media personalities who recommend Goldline http://www.goldline.com/goldline-testimonials
[6] Goldline Risk Disclosure; Coin Facts for Investors & Collectors to Consider http://www.goldline.com/buygold-investmentriskdisclosure

coins (e.g. Canadian Maple Leaf or South African Krugerrand gold coins) may range from approximately 5% to 20% depending on the coin though spreads may increase based upon market conditions, availability and demand. **Our spread on semi-numismatic coins, rare or numismatic coins and rare currency currently ranges from 30% to 35%. Examples of coins which have a 30% to 35% spread include European gold coins such as the Swiss 20 Franc, the PCGS certified "First Strike®" coins, coins which have been encapsulated by a grading service such as PCGS or NGC**, the Morgan and Peace silver dollars in all grades, and the Walking Liberty, Franklin and Kennedy silver half-dollars in all grades. Spreads may change based upon market conditions, availability and demand.

With the exception of the most common 1-ounce bullion coins, Goldline charges clients its numismatic spread, which currently ranges from 30% to 35%, on coins and currency. To earn a profit upon resale to us, your coins, currency or bullion must appreciate sufficiently to overcome this price differential.

To illustrate how this spread works, consider the following example. If the spread on a coin is 35% and Goldline's ask/sell price is $500 for the coin, then Goldline's bid/buy price is $325. Your coin must appreciate more than $175 to earn a profit. If you choose to sell your coin back to Goldline, you must also pay a 1% liquidation fee (the minimum liquidation fee is $15). Purchases of less than $1,500 are subject to a small lot fee of $15. *(Emphasis added)*

While this language may have been updated since I first included this statement in my 2010 book, these high commissions charged are typical of the industry. They say they will mail you information and the literature they send all leads the reader to high commissioned products. We don't send literature to clients as our website explains everything anyone needs to know to make a good decision. But quite frankly, if we did send literature we would lose money with our company policy of only selling the low commissioned bullion silver and gold products. Those gold dealers who advertise on TV and radio simply are making their money off of the high commissioned numismatic, rare and semi-rare coins they sell discussed in this chapter.

As the price of gold rises, more and more gold dealers will pop up to take advantage of the easy money to be made off unsuspecting buyers of gold. Ask anyone today to explain the gold market or how to go about buying gold coins, and most just can't don't know.

If insuring your portfolio against the fall or default of the U.S. economy or dollar is your intent, which would be the major reason to buy gold and silver bullion to begin with, then only buy bullion coins and bars.

Tactics Gold Dealers Use: Telling Buyers of Coins They Will Buy Them Back

Earlier, I gave you the question to ask all gold dealers who try and sell you rare or numismatic coins what they will buy the coins back for. You need to beware of the language they may try to use to confuse the buyer.

Some companies will tell investors they'll buy back the coins they purchase at just a 1% fee. This is a very attractive ploy to get people to buy. They'll sell the coins for $10,000 and tell the investor, "today we're just charging a 1% buyback fee." In the investor's mind, they're thinking $100. The reality of the situation is that it's 1% over their buy price, which is 15% to 30% less than what the investor purchased the coins for.

In the $10,000 example, the buyback price would be about $7,000 minus 1% or $6,930.

There are many articles on the internet offering advice on how to buy gold, what to buy and where to buy it. Most of these articles are written by marketers who are trying to funnel people into a marketing system of various information and products related to the gold industry, taking advantage of Google search engine page ranks. I have had several people ask me if they could use my book as part of their marketing system that also includes recommending rare coins. I have refused to go along with their request.

All investors in gold need is to ask the right questions and they will be buying gold and silver safely.

"In time of crisis, the common man won't appreciate any collector's value. What matters most is the gold weight."

—G. Edward Griffin

CHAPTER 9

Physical Gold - A Must For Every Portfolio and the Buying Gold Investment Grid

Worried investors who believe we're on the verge of an economic collapse are not just buying gold, they're buying gold and having it delivered. People do not trust the system and want the peace of mind that comes with owning gold they can touch.

All the added spending the government has conducted and continues to conduct will eventually have dire consequences on an already strained dollar. It is for this reason that investor must maintain a portfolio that at a minimum is 10% invested in physical gold coins and gold bars and not the paper alternatives or what many call substitutes for the real thing.

We aren't yet into that third euphoria stage of the gold bull market and are experiencing some volatility into 2018 beginning to appear with government shutdowns, but our government we cannot deny that Congress has an infatuation with debt, don't they? Remember when the dot com bull market was occurring? Everyone was saying people must get into dot com stocks. Into 2018 they are saying the same thing again. When people who were slow to act finally did get into dot com stocks, the dot com stocks crashed, some as much as 80%. They lost their shorts. In 2017 the leading dot com stocks, Facebook, Apple, Netflix and Google were up huge, but they didn't even have the earnings to justify the price growth.

A word of caution is needed here. If everyone and their brother is saying to get into gold, it might be time to take profit, depending on how the U.S. dollar is performing. But we're a long, long way away from that right now. **NOW is the time people need to investigate investing in physical gold and buying any dips that come, not adding the hope and dream potentials offered by dot com stocks with no growth in earnings to justify valuations.**

Supply and Demand

There's only so much gold mined each year and so much gold even in existence above ground and an even smaller amount below ground still to be mined as can be seen in the graphic below.

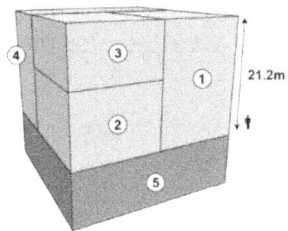

Total above ground stocks

Total above ground stocks: 187,200 tonnes
1 Jewellery: 89,200 tonnes, 47.6%
2 Private Investment: 40,000 tonnes, 21.4%
3 Official sector: 31,500 tonnes, 16.8%
4 Other: 26,500 tonnes, 14.2%
5 Below ground stocks: 57,000 tonnes
Source: GFMS, Thomson Reuters, US Geological Survey, World Gold Council

When gold is in demand, as the price moves higher, mints can't keep up with demand and there are shortages of metal, not just in the U.S. but the rest of the world like Germany, Austria, Canada France and Great Britain from mid-2005 to 2008 when prices took off. It will happen again once gold takes off. [1,2,3,4,5,6]

---

[1] Gold runs out in German rush, Allan Hall, London Evening Standard, Oct. 10, 2008 http://www.thisislondon.co.uk/standard-business/article-23571196-gold-runs-out-in-german-rush.do

[2] Austria witnesses new gold rush, Bethany Bell, BBC News, Vienna http://news.bbc.co.uk/2/hi/europe/7663753.stm

[3] Royal Canadian Mint under 'strain' to meet demand for gold, Eric Lam, October 3, 2008 http://network.nationalpost.com/np/blogs/fpposted/archive/2008/10/03/royal-canadian-mint-under-strain-to-meet-demand-for-gold.aspx

[4] Safe Option: Nervous French savers start gold rush, October 9, 2008 http://www.lankabusinessonline.com/fullstory.php?nid=18537900

[5] Market turmoil sends investors scrambling for gold, Richard Wray, guardian.co.uk, October 3, 2008
http://www.guardian.co.uk/business/2008/oct/01/commodities.creditcrunch

[6] Mint Widens Freeze on Gold Coin Sales - The Wall Street Journal http://online.wsj.com/article/SB122343298455514209.html?mod=googlenews_wsj
Gold Investment Grid http://bit.ly/GoldInvestmentGrid

The U.S. Mint in a memo dated August 15th, 2008 stated, "Due to the unprecedented demand for American Eagle gold 1-ounce 22-karat bullion coins, our inventories have been depleted. We are therefore temporarily suspending all sales of these coins."[7] They later resumed sales on a limited basis. The U.S. Mint is mandated by Congress to meet consumer demand, according to Public Law 99-185.22.[8] I see this as an issue for them when the real gold rush begins.

It is a long, tedious process to make these gold bullion coins, so the mints around the world just can't go out next week, make the coins and meet the demand of buyers everywhere.

When the U.S. Mint can't keep up, supply disappears and the premiums you pay for your coins also goes higher.

Reporting Requirements for Gold

What does a gold dealer report in purchase transactions to the IRS?

There is a lot of confusion in the gold industry about this. The industry in general is lazy on the subject and uses a memo from the 80's floating around and treats that memo like it is factual. In fact, it's all wrong as today the IRS is clear on what is reportable, but you have to do some digging to decipher the code. The answers as to what the code says follows;

Sales of precious metals. A sale of a precious metal
(gold, silver, platinum, or palladium) in any form for which
the Commodity Futures Trading Commission (CFTC) has
not approved trading by regulated futures contract (RFC)
is not reportable. Further, even if the sale is of a precious
metal in a form for which the CFTC has approved trading
by RFC, the sale is not reportable if the quantity, by weight

---

[7] Mint suspends red-hot Eagle gold coins
http://www.reuters.com/article/idUSN2140103820080821
[8] Public Law 99-185 Gold Bullion Coin Act of 1985
http://en.wikipedia.org/wiki/Gold_Bullion_Coin_Act_of_1985

or by number of items, is less than the minimum required quantity to satisfy a CFTC-approved RFC.

For example, a broker selling a single gold coin does not need to file Form 1099-B even if the coin is of such form and quality that it could be delivered to satisfy a CFTC-approved RFC if all CFTC-approved contracts for gold coins currently call for delivery of at least 25 coins.[9]

To understand what this means, you must find out what an RFC is.

For gold it is 100 troy ounces (not 25 which was the old contract in the 80's that is referred to by dealers so often). [10]

For silver it is 5,000 troy ounces.[11]

So, anything under 100 troy ounces for gold and 5,000 ounces for silver, is not reportable.

The code goes on to say;

Sales of precious metals for a single customer during a ~~24-hour period must be aggre~~gated and treated as a

---

[9] https://www.irs.gov/pub/irs-pdf/i1099b.pdf

[10] http://www.cmegroup.com/trading/metals/precious/silver_contract_specifications.html

[11] http://www.cmegroup.com/trading/metals/precious/silver_contract_specifications.html

single sale to determine if this exception applies. This exception does not apply if the broker knows or has reason to know that a customer, either alone or with a related person, is engaging in sales to avoid information reporting.

That first paragraph above (in quotes below) needs further clarification; "in any form for which the Commodity Futures Trading Commission (CFTC) has not approved trading by regulated futures contract (RFC) is not reportable."

To understand this more you need to know what silver "is" approved for an RFC.

To find that out you have to dig a little deeper and go to the NYMEX Rulebook

For Gold: Chapter 113 Gold Futures - Section 113101 CONTRACT SPECIFICATIONS.[12]
In a nutshell; 100 troy ounces of gold contract to be settled with either one 100 troy ounce bar (5% weight tolerance higher or lower) or 3 kilo bars.

For Silver; Chapter 112 Silver Futures - Section 112101 CONTRACT SPECIFICATIONS.[13]

In a nutshell: 5,000 troy ounces of silver contract is settled with five 1000-ounce bars (weight tolerance of 10% higher or lower).

In other words, for your average investor buying gold or silver today (probably 99.99% of you), there is NO reporting of any sale required

[12] http://www.cmegroup.com/rulebook/NYMEX/1a/113.pdf

[13] http://www.cmegroup.com/rulebook/NYMEX/1a/112.pdf

by a dealer. It should be noted that coins are not mentioned but one could assume more than 100 ounces of coins for gold and 5,000 ounces of coins for silver should be reported.

Reportable Item	Minimum Reportable Amount
Gold	More than 100 troy ounces
Silver	More than 5 - 1000 silver troy ounces

One should not be confused with this gold dealer reporting based on the size of purchase with the more than $10,000 cash reporting requirement by dealers. Any amount totaling **$10,000 or more of cash** for the purchase of gold or silver bars or coins **is reportable**. However, one could write a check for $1 million for gold (any amount) and it is not reportable. There is a lot of confusion out there on this $10,000 amount and it is only related to cash transactions. As a business practice, my company does not accept cash transactions and thus does not ever have to deal with the IRS on this issue. There are requirements of gold dealers to report any Anti Money Laundering activities.

Which Type of Gold Do I Recommend?

My philosophy is simple when it comes to buying gold and silver. Buy whatever is the lowest cost to the spot price of gold. The only products we sell are purely liquid gold and silver coins and bars. There is always a ready bid and ask to buy and sell the coins and bars just like there is a bid and ask for any listed stock on the exchange. You know before buying what we will buy it back for. As I said, if you don't know what the buyback price is for a coin or bar from a dealer is, ask them. Full liquidity when you need to sell or want to sell is what's important and only bullion gold bars and coins offer this liquidity.

Gold one-ounce bars are the most popular gold investment followed buy one-ounce gold Canadian Maple Leaf coins and the one-ounce gold American Eagle and American Buffalo coins. I rank these based on their cost to spot as well as liquidity factor. Yes, there are other coins and even larger size gold bars, but they just don't sell as much and aren't as liquid.

The Canadian Maple Leaf and U.S. gold coins have a higher premium to the gold bars, however their buy back prices are also higher. But why do you want to pay more for your gold? The best thing to do is to use that extra money that you would use to buy Canadian and U.S. Eagle or Buffalo coins and put it into buying more gold. But some investors like the idea of owning the Eagles and Buffalos.

Silver is covered in the silver section, but the same thing goes for silver, except the one-ounce rounds are less expensive than one-ounce bars, then 10-ounce bars and 100-ounce bars are the lowest cost, followed by the more expensive Canadian Maple and U.S. Eagles. However, U.S. Eagles Silver coins do make for a pretty gift to the younger generation to teach them about silver investing.

CHAPTER 10

How Do You Store Your Gold?

In times of monetary crisis, the most important aspect to owning gold will be, "how does one access their gold for purchases of necessities?"

The first rule in buying gold is to tell no one. Maybe tell a few family members who are at some point your heirs, but when/if times get tough, even friends may someday want some of the gold you own if they are aware of it. It's better to have peace of mind by keeping quiet about gold ownership. Don't let ego get in the way of survival. However, this doesn't mean you can't tell people the benefits and reasoning to own gold in helping them prepare for what troubles lay ahead. Just hand them this book or buy one for them. ☺

Safes

Diversify where the gold is stored. Keep some in secret places inside the home. I'm aware of some people who have more than one safe in their homes. The first one is put in a place like a closet or bedroom and contains some fake jewelry and maybe a little petty cash like one-dollar bills. These safes can be picked up for about $39.00 for the smaller ones, and larger combination safes for around $250.00.

If someone heard you had gold or if you are the unfortunate victim of a robbery, the first safe that would be easily found by a thief is just a substitute for the real safe kept hidden elsewhere. This first safe can contain some petty cash $1 bills, fool's gold coins that look real that you can buy online and other fake diamond rings and silver or gold jewelry you can buy online through eBay. Most thieves are not the smartest bunch and these items would get them out of your house. Some want to buy the big safes like the gun saves that no thief could drag out of the house. But if a thief put a gun to the head of someone you love, more than likely you would open the safe. If in trouble and threatened to give up the goods, gladly show them to this decoy safe and leave your guns for the gun safe only.

The real safe that you want hidden from thieves would preferably be a floor safe cemented into the ground and hidden somewhere, possibly under a refrigerator. You don't see movies of thieves checking out what's under the fridge, but you do see them looking in the freezer. However, if kept in a block of ice that no one can see through, hiding in plain sight may work. This real safe should be fireproof to avoid coins and bars from melting in case of fire. Floor safes will run anywhere from $300 to $700 or more.

You might be able to hide this safe behind a fake wall, although the expense of doing so might not be cost-effective. It depends on how much gold and silver one is hiding. Come up with your own unique ideas and know that it's not difficult to outsmart a thief.

Some people even go so far as to mark out an area with a Global Positioning Satellite (GPS) to secretly hide their gold in a place no one would ever look, like secluded woods or mountainous areas. They'll have to dig a little more than two feet to avoid the best metal detectors these days. There are always going to be prospectors hunting for stuff. It's a fun hobby for many. Anyone using this technique might want to rent a top-of-the-line metal detector to make sure the hoard can't be detected themselves. Naturally, it's best to be aware of your surroundings when going to bury it.

Safe Deposit Box

Many people believe one of the safest places to keep their gold is in their safe deposit box at a bank. This may be the only place for those who live in condos to store their metals. Bank holiday's may preclude you from getting to your wealth, so a few coins at home may be prudent.

While it is true that when a bank goes under they can't take the contents of your safe deposit box, you may not have access to the contents of the box until the government (FDIC) says you can have access to it. When it is needed most, it may not be available.

When the FDIC steps in to close a bank's operations, a depositor will not be able to withdraw cash, write checks or do anything with their funds inside that bank until the FDIC completes the transition to new ownership and funds are disbursed according to FDIC guidelines.

One thing people need to think about is, how can they prove what was in their safe deposit box? Can an owner file a claim on something they can't prove? Take pictures of everything inside the box and document it with a trusted witness.

While I'm not 100% against safe deposit boxes for storage, it is important that you maybe diversify your gold holdings. If one stash is found by someone who wasn't supposed to find it, there can be other places where you still maintain some wealth. As one grows older, they have to be aware that certain individuals will begin to pry into their finances and may take advantage of the elderly. I have even heard of phone calls to the parents of children from random people claiming to be their own child and from there sinister acts are forthcoming. Keep abreast of what your parents who are elderly are doing and if elderly, tell your trusted children what you are doing and what you have.

Are there any other problems associated with storing gold in Safe Deposit Boxes?

There is one glaring problem with safe deposit boxes these days, and that is banks have changed the rules and an owner must be aware that these changes could cause them to lose their gold.

If someone hasn't had contact with a bank for three years. Formerly, in some states like California, the bank could *legally* declare the property in the safe deposit box as "unclaimed" if it hasn't been touched in 3 years, sell the contents and put the proceeds into its general fund and possibly spend it. This is how it was in California until, recently when enough people complained, and the law was changed. The bank rules in your own state need to be known to prevent this from happening to your safe deposit box or even that of your parents who may not be aware of this and are storing valuables there that even you aren't aware of. It's time to have that conversation.

California now sends notices alerting citizens about unclaimed property before it is handed over to the state, *but it is the only state to do so*. Those who put their gold and silver in a safe deposit box need to find the potential future date that a state claims the box contents to be "unclaimed." Ask the bank president to answer that question.

If you're elderly, make sure children or a relative are aware of accounts owned. If you don't do this, who will know about it? I don't want to see the bank get anyone's assets just because they're afraid to discuss finances with family members. I am aware of an automatic withdrawal coming out of a deceased bank clients account no one was aware of in the family. The account paid for the monthly cost of the safety deposit box and when the account finally ran out of funds, the box was turned over to the state by the bank. Keep your family members informed.

Other Issues with Safe Deposit Boxes

To make matters worse, in England there was a raid on 7,000 safe deposit boxes, of which half were thought to be connected to criminal activity.[1] It's such an easy thing to do, especially if your safety deposit box has a lot of cash in it. Authorities were targeting criminals serving prison sentences or who were suspected criminals. During the raid, even if not part of the original, criminally-connected target boxes, the contents of other innocent owners' boxes could have gotten people in trouble. The raiding party will want to know where those contents came from, so keep documenting everything.

It will be up to the owner to prove the contents were acquired legally. This may not be easy for some to prove. Perhaps some purchases of gold coins under the 10k limit with the cash makes sense so you have a paper trail established.

---

[1] Police raid 7000 safety deposit boxes in blitz on British gangsters, Mirror.co.uk, February 6, 2008
http://www.mirror.co.uk/news/top-stories/2008/06/02/police-raid-7000-safety-deposit-boxes-in-blitz-on-british-gangsters-115875-20592803/

The raids are said to be continuing for many years. How long before this type of activity hits U.S. banks? Could there be an overreach by government should the economy go south? As the economy does deteriorate, the activity of the police state will increase. Three hundred officers were involved in the three cities in England where the raids occurred, and £1 billion of cash ($1.46 billion U.S.) went to the government.

Insuring Gold Stored at Home

Gold stored at home in a safe may or may not be covered as part of a "Personal Articles Insurance Policy," which is separate from a homeowner's policy. Some insurance companies do not cover gold bars. State Farm, for example, at the time of the first writing in 2010 only covered American Eagle gold coins, *not* gold bars. But that has changed this to not cover gold coins since 2010. Talk to your insurance agent and see what your policy will cover. On a side note, why do these insurance companies not cover gold and silver coins and bars which are easily valued and even Legal Tender for Eagles, when they cover gold, silver, and diamond jewelry and typically put a higher price on them than what they're worth? Some things just don't make sense.

The place you keep your gold at home is important to your insurance company as well. The gold must be kept in a steel combination lock safe that has a door that is at least one-inch thick and a body that is at least ½-inch thick. Again, talk to your insurance company before you buy a safe. Get the information in writing as to what is covered and what rules you need to follow and how often you should update the value of your investment. Last thing you want is for a theft to occur and your gold was valued far less than the going rate.

CHAPTER 11

Places to Purchase Physical Gold

There are many places where one can purchase gold. They can range from the local coin shop to those who advertise online or on radio or TV. We already know the tricks many of those who advertise on TV and radio play on investors). What you need to consider for purchases is not just where to buy, but also whether this company will be able to buy the gold you purchase back from you when it's time to sell. This is a question seldom discussed between the buyer and seller, but a very important one.

Many mints throughout the world, including the U.S. Mint, sell gold coins, but mostly commemorative and proof coins or high-priced bullion coins. Go ahead and check the U.S. Mint's website and you will find their market up on coins is quite high compare to most dealers.

Naturally, here in the United States, I will do what I can to offer the best price at the best place to buy metals through my company Buy Gold and Silver Safely. If for any reason I can't beat a price, I'll just tell you to buy. But of course, I would need to see who is offering it at a lower price online first.

But more than a salesman selling gold and silver, over the years I have been good at the timing of purchases in the articles I write as well. At times I will literally say I think we are due for a decline in price. My best advice for you is to buy the dips on a dollar cost average approach for your allocation percentage to gold and silver. Our business model is to simply look at all our competition and undercut them in price. It seems to work for us fine.[1]

---

[1] http://store.buygoldandsilversafely.com

Also, check the Better Business Bureau (BBB) in your area for complaints and ratings. But keep in mind, some companies that had "F" ratings simply changed their company status and now have an "A" rating by the BBB. They can change from an INC. to a LLC and it amazes me how the BBB allows this. As an alternative to BBB, Google "RipoffReport.com" as well to see if you can find any negative news on the company you are looking to purchase metals from. Also, many companies use TrustPilot for ratings. Yet many of these good reviews by buyers from some companies are pushed upon individuals just after the sale of the metals and the investor doesn't even know they have been ripped off yet. That's why I wrote this book, so you will know before buying metals, so you know that you won't get ripped off.

Ratings is big business and gold dealers have to pay BBB and TrustPilot money to get those reviews.

What can I use to purchase gold?

The following are the various ways you can purchase gold from a gold dealer:

Cash - Purchases of $10,000 or more in cash are subject to reporting requirements by the gold dealer. Successive purchases from the same gold dealer that add up to over $10,000 during a short period of time are subject to reporting requirements as well.

Checks with customer name on it - can take up to 10 business days to clear. Many gold dealers lock in the price up front buy may require a credit card to lock in the trade should prices fluctuate and the customer back out. The customer though will typically get the current price of gold at the time of purchase locked in which can benefit the customer in a moving market.

Checks drawn on foreign banks - may take up to 30 business days to clear.

Cashier's Checks – Ironically, if the cashier's check is over $10,000 there are no reporting requirements. But if you had 2 cashier's checks of $8,000 each that totaled over $10,000 ($16,000 in this example), and it is reportable. So, make your cashier checks over 10k and you're just fine.

Money Orders – treated same as cash and subject to $10,000 limit. Many gold dealers won't accept money orders because of the fraud associated with them.

Credit Card – extra fees are typically charged. These fees can be excessive, and I don't recommend using a credit card to purchase gold or silver. If you want miles for flying, try buying something else that doesn't have such a markup for use of credit.

Wired Funds - this is one of the fastest ways to purchase gold and the quickest way for you to get your metals. If the transaction is large, gold dealers will require the funds typically in 24 to 48 hours be wired in.

Shipping Concerns

Most gold dealers will ship your gold to you fully insured through FedEx, United Parcel Service (UPS) or the United States Postal Service (USPS). All have proven to be reliable and a very safe way to ship your purchase of gold or silver. Try and set up the delivery so you or someone you trust will be available to sign for it. Don't have the delivery set up so the package can be left on the doorstep. If it is insured, it must be signed for by an adult. I know of no gold dealers who ship this way to anyone without a signature required by an adult, so you should be fine here. A tracking number is sent to you in advance and you can follow it all the way to your doorstep. For larger orders, companies like Brinks may deliver in an armored car to a business address only.

It is important to note that silver is very heavy, and you should have someone strong enough to help move the larger purchases if taking delivery. Silver I like better for IRA's, so you don't have to worry about delivery.

Also, when it comes time to selling it back, you'll have to package the metals and ship back to the dealer. The best way I have found to do that is through USPS Registered Insured.

CHAPTER 12
Investing in Gold with an IRA or 401(k)

Most people don't know they can rollover or transfer some of their IRA or a 401k and invest in physical gold and silver coins and bars. There are several companies that allow you to set up what's called a self-directed IRA, which allows you to invest directly in physical gold and silver.

There are several self-directed IRA companies. The Entrust Group, GoldStar Trust, Equity Institutional, New Direction are four of the most popular.

An example of how a self-directed IRA works:

> The process starts by the IRA investor completing paperwork with the self-directed IRA company and transferring funds there via an IRA rollover or IRA transfer. Once the funds are in-house (transferred), the gold dealer is contacted to purchase the metals. The metals would be shipped from the gold dealer/supplier to the new depository or storage facility in the name of the IRA holder with an account number for reference. The gold would be held at the depository in an allocated or unallocated account (depending on how you set it up) until the day it is sold or shipped to the IRA holder if they decide to make withdrawals or are forced to at age 70 ½. Taxes of course would have to be paid on any funds withdrawn.

There are only certain gold and silver investments that can be put into a precious metals IRA. The following graphic explains.

Precious metals can be held in your IRA in the following forms:

Gold

- American Eagle coins(1)
- American Buffalo coins(2)
- Australian Kangaroo/Nugget coins
- Austrian Philharmonic coins
- Canadian Maple Leaf coins
- Bars and rounds produced by a refiner/assayer/manufacturer accredited by NYMEX/COMEX, NYSE/Liffe, LME, LBMA, ISO 9000, or national government mint and meeting minimum fineness requirements(3)(4)

Silver

- American Eagle bullion and proof coins(1)
- Australian Kookaburra coins
- Austrian Philharmonic coins
- Canadian Maple Leaf coins
- Mexican Libertad coins
- Bars and rounds produced by a refiner/assayer/manufacturer accredited by NYMEX/COMEX, NYSE/Liffe, LME, LBMA, ISO 9000, or national government mint and meeting minimum fineness requirements(3)(4)

1. Numismatic and American Eagle coins that have undergone "certification" (also known as "slabbed" coins) are not acceptable in IRAs at this time.
2. Only uncirculated type American Buffalo coins are allowed (i.e. no Proof coins are allowed).
3. Minimum Fineness Required: Gold .995+ Silver .999+ Platinum .9995+ Palladium .9995+
4. Small bullion bars (i.e. bars other than 400-ounce gold, 100-ounce gold, 1000-ounce silver, 50-ounce platinum, and 100-ounce palladium bars) must be manufactured to exact weight specifications.

The unscrupulous gold dealers have found a way to include the high commission 1.5-ounce silver coins like the Grizzly Bear coin in your IRA, so watch out for these companies pushing you towards these coins.

The least expensive way to own gold in an IRA is to own the gold with the smallest spread. This would be the higher weight bars like a kilo bar. Many prefer coins though in an IRA simply because they want to start taking out a distribution and not have to sell an entire bar for a partial or mandatory withdrawal. Make sure you have some coins or bars for liquidity purposes.

My recommendation would be to diversify the percentage of gold allocated to the IRA with 50% put in 1-ounce gold bars and 50% in 1-ounce silver rounds. But I will say this from an investment standpoint, I think silver can double before gold does in the years that come. Once the silver investment does double you can sell half of it and use those proceeds to buy the more stable gold bars.

As an example, if silver was $20 an ounce, it would $40 an ounce and still be under its all-time high. If gold doubled from $1,300, it would be well above its all-time high. We'll discuss more on the gold/silver ratio to see what investment makes sense to go overweight in a later chapter.

But there is another rip-off for IRA's that gold dealers do. Of all the possible choices for putting gold and silver into an IRA, gold dealers will push the "proof" coins on the unsuspecting investor because they offer the salesperson a higher commission, up to 30%. Understand this is their nature and the ownership of these large gold dealers push their salesmen and women to put investors into these proof coins or even the 1.5-ounce silver coins because of the big commissions.

In fact, I challenge you to do your own experiment and call these gold dealers up and see what they recommend. You'll simply never hear them say bullion gold and silver coins or bars as an answer. And play the experiment out with them and ask what they buy back the gold and silver proof coins and sets and the 1.5-ounce silver coins back for if you sold them back to them the same day at the same spot price. These companies need to be exposed for what they do. But unfortunately, most investors who buy these proof coins and 1.5-ounce coins don't know they are getting ripped off.

I was interviewed for a Wall Street Journal article and went back and forth with the editor for 2 months as he was investigating the sale of proof coins by gold dealers. I mentioned to him that the 1.5-ounce coins were being offered as a coin where they are ripping clients off and in the story, he didn't mention one thing about it. Why? Because the gold dealer that was doing the most abusing was advertising on the television shows of the company that owns the Wall St. Journal. Let me tell you this flat out; every company that advertises on TV is ripping you off. Just call them and ask the questions above that I gave you. Someday, someone will write the truth.

I was also interviewed by AARP magazine and mentioned it to them how gold dealer's rip-off clients, and they wrote nothing about it. See what kind of non-sense you are up against?

Lately some gold dealers are starting to charge clients up to 30% even on the gold and silver bullion put into an IRA in a blatant attempt to capitalize on ignorance of investing in metals. Don't give in to these greedy salespeople. Know what to do before investing.

Get copies of the application you signed to make sure the sales representative didn't check off the "proof" box with a higher spread or charge you more than agreed upon for the gold you purchased. Don't assume they are telling you the truth. Notify them immediately of any issues.

Be aware that some gold dealers will quote the price of bullion gold, not tell you the spread, and just want to get the money in-house. Once the money is in-house, an IRA specialist will get on the phone and discuss the various options which of course include the proof coins or something else with higher commissions. They are relentless.

If the salesperson balks, take your business elsewhere. The money is now with the IRA custodian and you can pick whichever gold dealer will give you the best price. It's your money, not theirs! Just make sure the new gold dealer is listed on the application and the other one removed. There will be a form you sign for this.

The distribution of coins, whether from an IRA can take two to four weeks, but a seller will be given the price quoted at the time of request for redemption. That's nice because you can sell with just a phone call to the gold dealer.

If things get bad for the economy one can always take possession of the metals inside the IRA at any point in time, but again, would have to pay taxes. They can even drive up to where the metals are held and literally, back up the truck and take delivery. Prior arrangements must be made.

Gold and Silver In a 401(k) – Now Available

Most 401(k) plans in America don't allow individuals to invest in physical metals through their 401(k). Why is that? The reason is most

401(k)s are funded by the big investment wire houses, who don't want outside competition to their securities products like mutual funds and ETFs. Today you can add physical gold and silver as an additional option for your 401(k) if your employer or operations approves it. Or once you separate yourself from the company by retirement or other reasons, you can roll some or all of the IRA into the self-directed company to invest in precious metals.

For IRA's, keep in mind that you are only allowed to do one rollover every calendar year but can do as many transfers from institution to institution as you want.

CHAPTER 13
Where to Sell Gold

If you do a search on Google for where to sell your gold, you'll find many dealers willing to buy. **The best place to sell gold however, will probably be where it was purchased from.** But call around and check out who is offering the best price. If you start with a reputable dealer to buy your metals after using the information from this book, whether you do business with Buy Gold and Silver Safely or not, you'll avoid getting ripped off. The reason we choose to sell only bullion gold and silver bars and coins is because it is the most liquid. There is always going to be a buyer for bullion. These bullions coins and bars won't be difficult to sell. The timing of when to sell though, is something we can help with.

PART II - SILVER

Chapter 14
<u>Silver: The Other Precious Metal</u>

Silver offers investors a similar opportunity as gold for diversification of portfolios, as it too has counteracted the decline of the U.S. dollar. What's important to note about the silver section is that it is briefer than the gold section, simply because I told you that I would use the words "gold" to include both gold and silver throughout the book. They move in tandem in price with silver having a bit more volatility.

You'll recall our 1964 quarter that is 90% silver purchasing power exchanged for the scrip of the day to buy things, versus the 1965 quarter that buys you 25 cents worth of things today. Most in the U.S. can't even see what the government has done to our money and yes, most don't know anything about how silver over time maintains its purchasing power. Silver has an additional benefit, as it is utilized as an industrial metal and this can make it at times in higher demand than gold. Silver can also be more volatile than gold and the timing of its purchase and sale is important. This volatility can present some good opportunities for profit if the timing is right.

Silver is hardly ever mentioned in the financial media. Yet for some odd reason, our founding fathers decided to mention it in the Constitution.

Perhaps the reason our founding fathers saw fit to include silver along with gold in the Constitution is because silver has been money since the times when Judas was given 30 pieces to deliver Jesus to the high priests. There's a long history as money backing it.

The Temple Tax Coin, Tyre KP Type Half Shekel, Jerusalem or Tyre Mint, 14 - 15 A.D.[1]

History of Silver as Money

The silver penny, or pound sterling, was in use for 1,100 years and served as the predominant source of coinage.

In the early years of the United States, the colonies would use silver coins known as Pieces of Eight (Spanish Reales or Spanish Dollars) as a medium of exchange that circulated along with other coins made of copper or gold.

In 1792, with the approval of Thomas Jefferson and George Washington, the Spanish Dollar became legal tender through the Coinage Act of 1792.[2]

There were attempts to create banks in the U.S., but they didn't last long. The First Bank of the United States (1791) lasted four years (although its charter was until 1811) but had a relevant decree to "neither issue notes nor incur debts beyond its actual capitalization."[3] Can you imagine if this stayed true? Well, we wouldn't have been able to fund many things, so it's a whole different subject, but it is true that

---

[1] Judas' 30 Pieces of Silver - Matthew 26:14-15 – FORVM Ancient Coins
http://www.forumancientcoins.com/catalog/roman-and-greek-coins.asp?vpar=808
[2] Coinage Act of 1792 Wikipedia -
http://en.wikipedia.org/wiki/Coinage_Act_of_1792
[3] First Bank of the United States Wikipedia -
http://en.wikipedia.org/wiki/First_Bank_of_the_United_States

there have been tremendous benefits from some debt the government has carried. They have just taken it too far.

The Second Bank of the United States (1816 - 1836) was established primarily because the U.S. was having difficulty financing the war of 1812 and its aftermath.[4] Once again, going into debt to finance wars is and should be accepted. Of course, the Constitution dictates the wars be declared by Congress and we haven't had that since WWII.

President Andrew Jackson wasn't happy about what was going on with the 2nd bank. He saw it as "an instrument of political corruption and a threat to American liberties."[5] The banks were running out of gold but tried to renew their charter four years early and ran into a brick wall in President Jackson.[6]

Silver remained legal tender until its 1857 demonetization resulting from the discovery of gold in California.

It was the discovery of gold in California, coupled with the discovery of even more gold in Alaska that resulted in the doubling of the world's gold supplies by 1900. This laid the groundwork for the Gold Standard Act and the demise of silver.[7]

But it was also the bankers who were upset. They didn't like the fact that citizens could take their silver discoveries down to the Mint and have them turned into coins for their own personal use. In other words, they couldn't get a piece of the action. This according to Martin Wetzel Walbert, author of the 1899 book *The Coming Battle: A Complete History of the National Banking Money Power in the United States*.[8]

From the book:

---

[4] Second Bank of the United States - http://en.wikipedia.org/wiki/Second_bank_of_the_united_states
[5] Andrew Jackson Congressional record, Vol. 78, Jan. 15, 1934, pp. 614-615
[6] Andrew Jackson addressing the 2nd Bank of the US (1832)
[7] Gold Standard Act http://en.wikipedia.org/wiki/Gold_Standard_Act
[8] The Coming Battle: A Complete History of the National Banking Money Power in the United States. Chapter III: National Banks and Silver, Martin Wetzel Walbert (1899) http://web.archive.org/web/19990427115804/lvdi.net/~willys/cbtabcon.htm

> The owner of silver could take his bullion to the mint, have it coined into standard silver dollars of full legal tender debt, paying power, receive them after their mintage, and transact business by their means; he was not under the necessity, when in need of money, to make application to a national bank for a loan of its circulating notes, whose sole credit rested on the solvency of the United States. He was not compelled to pay toll to the national banks for the use of their debts as money.
>
> The national banking money power could not control the silver dollar, as long as the law authorized its free coinage, and consequently, a gigantic conspiracy was formed in London and New York City to demonetize silver.
>
> This great money power whose almost absolute control of the currency was surely driving all business to a credit basis, deliberately planned the destruction of that precious metal whose value has been far more stable than that of gold.

You see how this works with government and bankers, right?

In 1913, the bankers were up to their tricks again, and they passed the Federal Reserve Act as the result of a secret meeting by bankers and businessmen at Jekyll Island, Georgia.[9,10]

This Act introduced Federal Reserve Notes to the public for the first time. Twenty short years later, President Franklin Roosevelt would confiscate the U.S. citizens' gold, as discussed earlier in the book. The gold was then used to make the government's financial balance sheet stronger by artificially raising the price of it.

But silver wasn't confiscated. Silver was still an afterthought because of all the gold that was discovered in California and Alaska, and the fact that bankers didn't want anyone to consider it money. The bankers you remember didn't want any new discoveries of silver to be brought in to the Mint to make coins. They would have just preferred silver disappeared altogether as the bankers have a new game to play with fiat money they could create out of thin air.

But President Roosevelt had this to say about silver in a message to Congress, January 15, 1934:[11]

---

[9] Federal Reserve Act http://www.federalreserve.gov/aboutthefed/fract.htm
[10] The Creature from Jekyll Island, G. Edward Griffin
http://www.amazon.com/Creature-Jekyll-Island-Federal-Reserve/dp/0912986212

"The other principal precious metal— silver—has also been used from time immemorial as a metallic base for currencies as well as for actual currency itself. It is used as such by probably half the population of the world. It constitutes a very important part of our own monetary structure. It is such a crucial factor in much of the world's international trade that it cannot be neglected."

President Roosevelt even laid down the amount of silver the government should keep on hand in May of 1934:[12]

"I, therefore, recommend legislation at the present session declaring it to be the policy of the United States to increase the amount of silver in our monetary stocks with the ultimate objective of having and maintaining one fourth of their monetary value in silver and three fourths in gold."

After gold was confiscated by the U.S. government in 1933, there were primarily two paper currencies that the people could choose from: Federal Reserve Notes (94% of the currency), issued by Federal Reserve Banks and Silver Certificates, issued by the U.S. Treasury.
From the Federal Reserve, *A Primer on Money*, 1964:[13]

What backs the Federal Reserve Notes?

Behind the Federal Reserve notes is the credit of the U.S. government. If you happen to have a $5, $10, or $20 Federal Reserve note, you will notice across the top of the bill a printed statement of the fact that the U.S. government promises to pay, not that the Federal Reserve promises to pay. Nevertheless, most Americans don't realize what the government promises to pay: American citizens holding these notes cannot demand anything for them except (a) that they be exchanged for other Federal Reserve notes, or (b) that they be accepted in payment for taxes and all

---

[11] Message to Congress Recommending Legislation on the Currency System. January 15, 1934 http://www.presidency.ucsb.edu/ws/index.php?pid=14868
[12] FDR's message to Congress of May 22, 1934 Recommending Legislation on Silver (from Congressional Record, Vol. 78, May 22, 1934, pp. 9209-10)
[13] Subcommittee on Domestic Finance; Committee on Banking and Currency, House of Representatives – 88th Congress 2d Session – August 5, 1964

debts, public and private. Certain official or semiofficial foreign banks may exchange any "dollar credits" they may hold—that is, deposits with the commercial banks—for an equal amount of the Treasury's gold. Americans themselves may not exchange them for gold. But because, in commerce with foreign nations, Americans may pay in gold, gold actually "backs" American dollars.

What backs the Treasury currency?

   The Treasury currency in circulation today is largely silver certificates. By law, the government requires the Treasury to keep on deposit a certain amount of silver to "back" silver certificates. The Treasury must do the same for the Treasury notes of 1890. This means that anyone holding silver certificates can obtain silver for them on demand. The Treasury's legal reserve of silver amounts to about two-thirds the value of the silver certificates in circulation.

To recap the above, Federal Reserve Notes are backed by the *credit* of the U.S. government, and ultimately, they conclude that "gold" backs them and Silver Certificates are backed by silver.

Silver coins continued to circulate in the U.S. with the production of 1-ounce coins ending in 1935. Silver dimes, quarters and half-dollars continued to circulate until 1964, when silver was removed from all dimes and quarters, and half-dollars' silver content was reduced to 40%.

Flash forward a few years and in 1968, the government refused to pay any more silver to bearers of Silver Certificates. In other words, they became worthless.

In 1969, the government stopped producing 40% silver half-dollars all together. Bankers finally win the battle over silver.

Two years after that in 1971, as was pointed out in Chapter 1, President Nixon took the United States off any metal standard completely. Bankers finally win the battle over gold.

"The truth is that all men having power ought to be mistrusted."

—James Madison, Father of the Constitution

Chapter 15
Silver Uses, Supply and Demand[1]

Now that we know what the monetary value of silver has been in history, and what those in power like to do to it to keep it from being viewed as money (a store of value which is all we citizens want), we need to look at silver in another light, as an industrial metal.

When it comes to analyzing the uses of silver, one must keep in mind that while there are many new uses for silver, the demand has also decreased in photography, historically one of the biggest industry users of silver. But it has picked up in other uses related to technology and continues to do so.

According to Geology.com;

> Silver is a precious metal because it is rare and valuable, and it is a noble metal because it resists corrosion and oxidation, though not as well as gold. Because it is the best thermal and electrical conductor of all the metals, silver is ideal for electrical applications. Its antimicrobial, non-toxic qualities make it useful in medicine and consumer products. Its high luster and reflectivity make it perfect for jewelry, silverware, and mirrors. Its malleability, which allows it to be flattened into sheets, and ductility, which allows it to be drawn into thin, flexible wire, make it the best choice for numerous industrial applications. Meanwhile, its photosensitivity has given it a place in film photography. [2]

For those that think the U.S. is headed to more wars, during World War II, silver was used for machine tools, electrical and other functions related to the production of war goods. Silver during WWII increased in price by 36%.

---

[1] All Silver Usage and Mining data derived from CPM Group's Silver Yearbook 2009 with 2010 figures updated separately. Used with permission from Jeffrey Christian, Managing Director http://store.cpmgroup.com/agyb2009.html
[2] http://geology.com/articles/uses-of-silver/

During WWII, silver prices rose for several reasons. One was in fact the heavy use of silver in the war effort. One of the biggest uses then was in reconnaissance photography, as well as in electronics, and various heating and cooling systems. Silver also was heavily relied upon as an alternative to currencies during the war, with the US government lending and shipping enormous volumes, hundreds of millions of ounces, of silver coins and bars to China, India, Middle Eastern countries and regions, and other regions for use as a currency and in trade during a time when the international currencies system was not working well and silver was more acceptable in various forms of commerce than money.[3]

David Morgan, a well-known silver analyst, claims that demand in silver with "many up-and-coming 'green' technologies like photovoltaic cells in solar arrays that require silver coatings, water-purification plants that use silver compounds to prevent bacteria and algae buildup, super-efficient, eco-friendly silver-zinc batteries may soon supplant their lithium-ion cousin in the rapidly growing electric car market."[4]

The auto industry may also soon take advantage of silver-zinc batteries.

"Silver oxide batteries, also known as silver–zinc batteries, provide up to 40% more run time than lithium-ion batteries. Over 95% of key battery elements can be recycled and reused and they utilize a water-based chemistry that is free from the thermal runaway and flammability problems that have plagued the lithium-ion alternatives," according to Zpower.[5]

Zpower is all set to use silver-zinc batteries for the next generation of notebook computers, cell phones and consumer electronics.[6]

---

[3] Jeffrey Christian, Managing Director CPM Group in personal email to author
[4] David Morgan: A Bull's Case For Silver, Lara Crigger, April 29, 2009
http://www.hardassetsinvestor.com/features-and-interviews/1/1544-david-morgan-a-bulls-case-for-silver.html
[5] ZPower http://www.zincmatrixpower.com/index.htm
[6] ZPower next generation silver uses
http://www.zincmatrixpower.com/applications/index.htm

Buy Gold and Silver Safely

The military has used silver-zinc batteries in missiles, torpedoes and submarines for over 50 years. It's kind of easy to do if you have an almost unlimited budget of taxpayer money.

The top 3 areas of use for silver are Industrial Applications, Jewelry & Silverware and lastly for investment purposes, Coins & Bars. The investment demand for silver has fallen since 2015 and was even lower into 2018 with the Trump election. U.S. Mint sales crashed. But demand in the other areas has stayed steady.

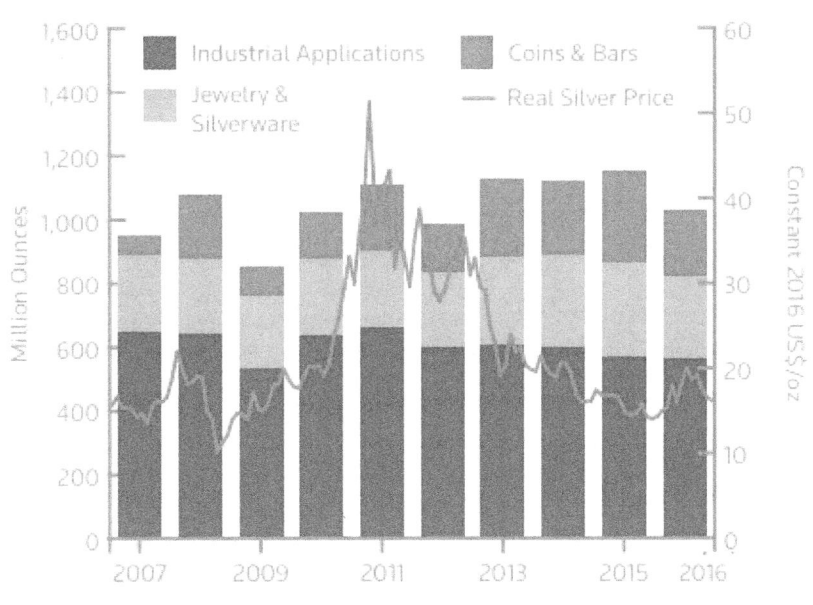

Source: GFMS, Thomson Reuters

U.S. Mint sales for 2016 were $37,701,500 and were cut in half in 2017, down to 18,065,500.

Some investors are seeing the writing on the wall with this economy and buying coins and bars on the cheap. As industry looks for more uses, the price is surely to go higher even without the government screwing things up.

Investment demand is not just coming from North America, but also India, Europe and China as seen in the following chart.

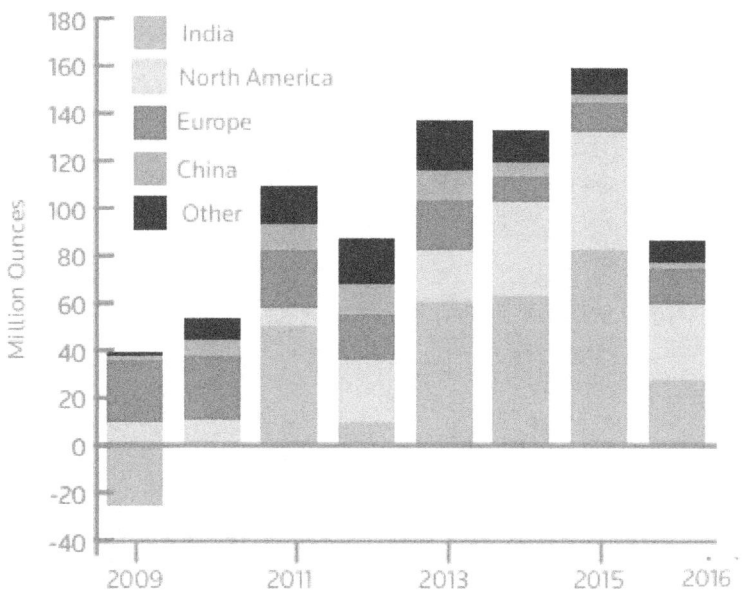

Source: GFMS, Thomson Reuters

Silver Supply

According to the 2017 World Silver Survey, the production of silver has increased almost every year since 2005 but the overall supply has held steady the last 6 years. One thing that stopped 6 years ago was the net government sales. The government has no silver today except for what is mandated to the U.S. Mint to obey the laws laid down for production of American Eagles as discussed before.

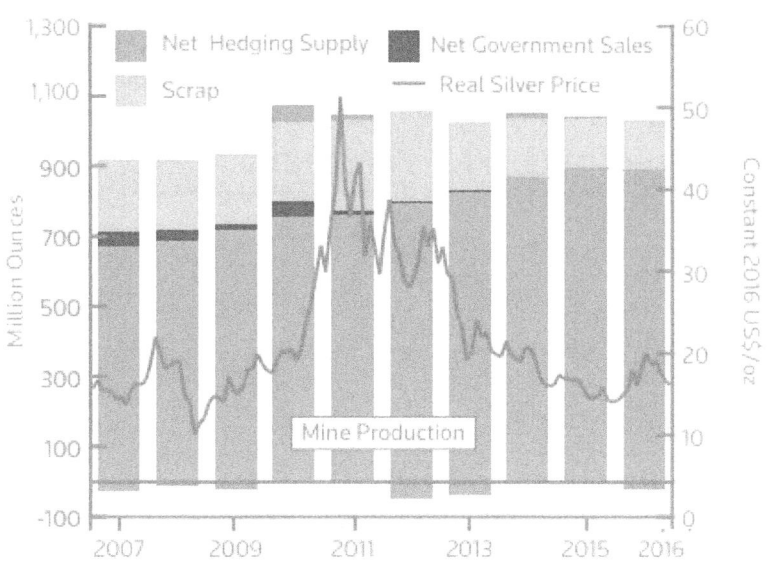

Government Stockpiles

The government sold most of its silver from 1999-2013, which ranks them right up there with the central banks of the world as far as having good timing. They sold the entire time the price went higher. From the World Silver Survey 2017;

> There is little publicly available data on the level of government silver stocks and accordingly assessments of these are largely based on private information gathered during the course of our field research. There were only minimal sales in the early part of this decade and we estimate none at all have taken place in 2014, 2015 or 2016. While our field research indicates no activity at all, even if a small transaction did take place it would have been at an inconsequential level when compared to

the previous fifteen years when disposals averaged 48 M oz (1,392 t) per annum over the 1999-2013 period. At end 2016, total government silver stocks amounted to 89.1 M oz (2,771 t).

Producer Hedging on the Decline

One area that will push the price of silver higher and faster, is there is not going to be as much big money pushing it down to protect themselves from the falling price of silver, otherwise known as hedging. With fewer hedges, there is less manipulation and the price of silver can freely rise.

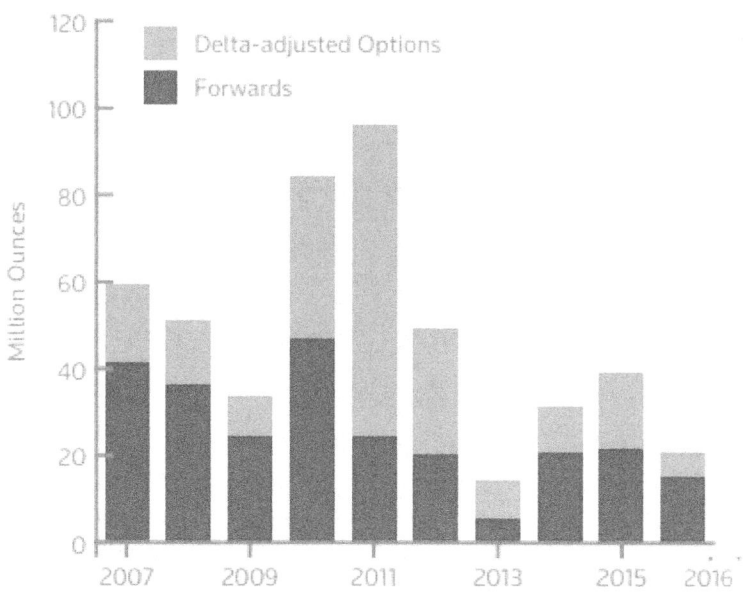

Silver ETFs

Silver ETFs are another place where demand for silver is coming from. Silver ETFs started trading in mid-2006. The use of ETFs for buying silver may be good for trading, but it does not offer an investor the ability to take delivery of the metal and is not cost effective for the one's that allow as discussed earlier. The most popular silver ETF and largest is SLV. Of course, how is the custodian of it but none other than JP Morgan Chase bank. I think I'll pass. But any Google search can find you some ETFs to trade. Just check the prospectus and don't look at them as a substitute for holding physical silver.

Conclusion

The price of silver was $9.10 an ounce in 2005, yet despite the decrease in demand and increase in production and secondary supply since then, the price climbed to around $14 in 2009 and over $19 in 2010. Production even increased, and investment demand stayed the same since and silver still hit a high of 49.50 in 2011, 50 cents from its all-time high. It will get there again and more.

Silver's relationship to fiat currencies as a store of value is proven over time. It is the U.S. dollar value of silver that has increased. It is the fact that silver represents *real* wealth, and conversely the U.S. dollar represents *perceived* wealth that investors are concerned with. It is this mindset of the individual that is the difference. Silver is money. And over time that 1964 quarter will more than likely buy you a gallon of gas when exchanged for the scrip of the day.

The Importance of Retiring with Wealth

The first Baby Boomer applied for Social Security in 2007. How great it is that Boomers who have paid into Social Security can finally start reaping the income from their hard work over the years!

But are they getting a fair shake?

The whole Social Security system is based on one thing, and that is that the dollars you put into the system in the early years will be able to buy goods and services when you finally start receiving checks in your retirement years. When government is left to run the show, can you really expect to get a fair deal?

The dollar the first Baby Boomer put into the Social Security system in 1963 at age 18 would have bought you about 20 candy bars, 20 stamps, or four gallons of gas. Today, what will that dollar buy them? Unfortunately, the game was rigged against them from the beginning.

I'm a Baby Boomer. I can remember when candy bars cost five cents. I told myself when they raised the price to 10 cents, I would never buy a candy bar again. That lasted for a while, but a kid can only refrain from sweets for so long!

Flash forward to today, and the checks Boomers receive from Social Security will continue to buy less if the government continues to spend beyond their means. Eventually higher prices will arrive because of all the pumping of money into the system by the Federal Reserve and our government. Stocking away some money in silver just makes sense.

But it is the potential collapse of the system that implores people to buy silver. Silver, along with gold, are poised to help investors. Silver and gold will always have purchasing power value and provide the wealth needed as the U.S. dollar struggles with the debt load that never seems to end.

Chapter 16

Silver Is Money Today

Some may say that silver is no longer money, but the charts sure tell a different story. While silver is used as an industrial metal the world over, it still reacts inversely to the dollar, despite supply and demand ramifications, as seen in the following chart.

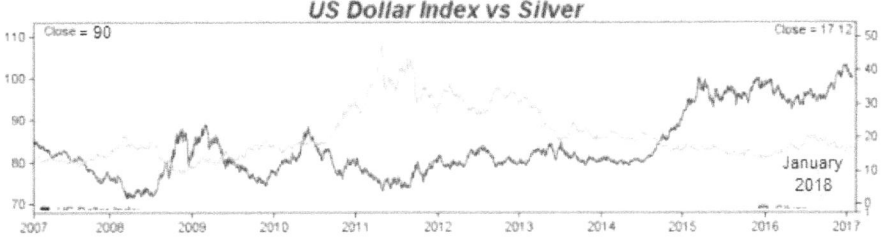

Over time, the inverse relationship of silver and the dollar is shown to be accurate (emphasis on "over time." Right now, in my humble opinion, is the time to be buying. The evidence of this book dictates such.

What in one's investment portfolio do investors have to protect themselves from the deterioration of the U.S. dollar if it were to decline more into the future because of government spending madness? What else has this type of track record?

Silver at present is offering one of the best opportunities where an investor can preserve their wealth and at the same time profit.

A silver investment allows you to take control of your financial planning and offers the best hedge, along with gold, against government and Fed Monopoly games with the banks.

Remember playing the board game Monopoly? Who was the loser in that game? It was always the person mortgaging their property to the hilt. Even the player who spent all their money on houses and hotels and was cash-poor had to do sell those houses and hotels at half-price to raise cash and pay the owner.

When the Fed announced in March of 2009 that they would buy up to $300 billion in long-term Treasuries over the next six months, and that they would broaden the Fed's balance sheet with the purchase of $1.25 trillion of mortgage-backed securities, they were essentially doing what the losing Monopoly player does... except they were also the banker. The truth is found not in their ability to be banker and buyer, but in what real money did the day the Fed went on its spending spree.

What did the price of silver do that day?[1] It went from $12.95 to $13.68 in one day, a 5% increase, as seen in the next chart.

This dramatic move in the price of silver is proof-positive that silver is viewed as a safe haven when the Fed exposes its hand.

In a sense, the Fed is and will continue trying to bail themselves out of the mess they got themselves into, time and time again as the buyer of last resort. It is they and the bankers who should "go to jail, go directly to jail, do not pass Go, and stop confiscating any more of the people's wealth!"

I can't finish this thought though until I tell you what is exactly in the monopoly game rules (look it up).

---

[1] Fed to Buy $300 Billion of Longer-Term Treasuries, Bloomberg, March 18, 2009 http://www.bloomberg.com/apps/news?pid=20601087&sid=ai9ygzsBdynw&refer=home

"The Bank never "goes broke." If the Bank runs out of money, the Banker may issue as much more as may be needed by writing on any ordinary paper."

Isn't it ironic that the Monopoly game came out in 1934, one year after President Roosevelt confiscated the gold and devalued the dollar?

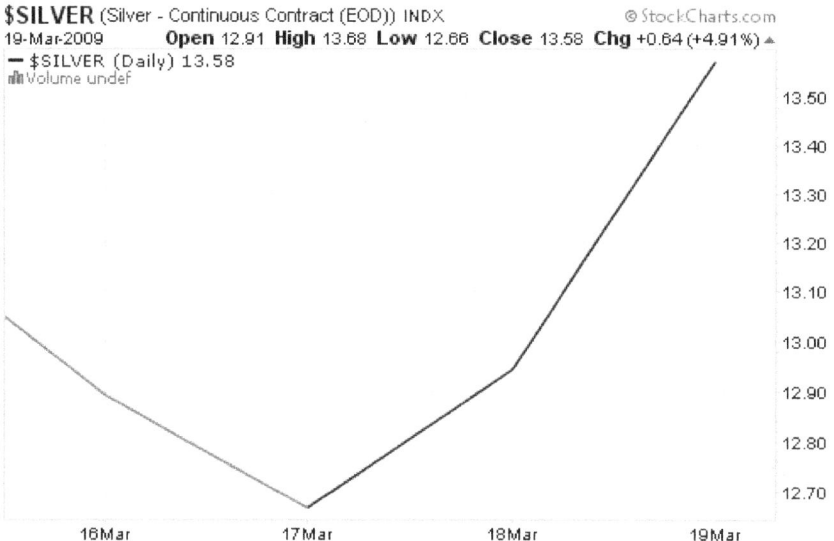

The truth is, this "game" the government and the Fed are playing with the fruits of one's labor needs insurance, and gold and silver are the only assets that offer such insurance to a declining dollar. This is how you win the game.

But what is the best buy price for silver? Ideally, depending on when you are reading this book, it is if during a deflationary collapse we fall to the $10-$15 range. You can see where this is the base for silver in the following chart.

If you are reading this book after 5 years from the latest update, then you may see the price of silver already higher. More than likely that 1964 90% silver quarter dollar can still buy you a gallon of gas no matter when you buy it (exchanged for the scrip of the day), but you'll be able to keep abreast of what I think about silver through my weekly comments on the blog over at:

http://buygoldandsilversafely.com/category/current-thoughts/

CHAPTER 17
Gold/Silver Ratios

To understand the ratio of the prices of gold and silver, let's look at an example. If the price of gold were $1,000 an ounce and the price of silver $20, the ratio would be 1000/20 = 50. What "50" represents is that gold is 50 times more valuable than silver.

Historical ratios of gold and silver have fluctuated between 12:1 and 16:1 but the monthly gold/silver ratio has been 30:1 to 100:1 over the past 30 years. Since May of 2009 it has remained steady with a slight increase to just over 80 in 2016 and settling in at the 75/76 range in 2017 and slightly higher around 78 heading into the beginning months of 2018.

You can see an example of the ratio falling and how silver gains strength during this time in the graphic that follow.

The line in the sand for the gold/silver ratio seems to be 75:1 to 80:1 and a good time to be buying silver based on the historical patterns below. There of course can be overshoots as in 1991 and 2011 but a reversion to the 60 level seems to be the next stop. Silver in the beginning of 2018 should outperform gold and this ratio should be on its way to 60 or lower.

CHAPTER 18

Types of Silver to Invest In

Because of the weight of silver versus gold, buying a monster box (500 ounces) of silver coins would weigh approximately 31 lbs. Imagine taking delivery of $100,000 worth of silver. It's a heavy metal.

Silver is a different animal from gold when it comes to cost and weight, but there are some specific recommendations you need to adhere to in acquiring silver. The following analysis only includes those silver investments that the average investor can profit from without paying the high commissions of what is normally sold by gold dealers as discussed in Chapter 8.

Physical Silver

What's important to the buyer when acquiring silver is how much they will pay over the spot price, also known as the premium or spread. The issue though is that the premiums on coins and bars fluctuate based on supply and demand. When mints or dealers run out of certain products, the premiums rise. Also, as the price rises, the premium typically rises too. Let's address the premium issue first.

Premium Fluctuation with Silver Products

As the price of silver falls, sometimes the premiums rise because typically a gold supplier will buy silver in advance from the mint's, so they have an adequate supply to meet demand. If for some reason they haven't hedged their purchase from the potential of falling prices, or if a fast drop occurs and their hedges are not enough, then they don't have a choice on what to do to protect themselves and therefore raise the premiums on the coins to compensate. After a while premiums recover back to normal. Remember, the suppliers to gold dealers are not in the business of losing money. They will do whatever it takes to protect the bottom line.

We could see some big swings in just days in the future with silver. It has happened in the past and will again. But we aren't near those big swings till we get closer to the $50 market again. We will have to look over at the dollar and other economic conditions to understand if silver is worth holding onto for a longer period. More than likely it will be as we sure as heck know that when interest rates shoot up and the interest on the debt will be difficult to pay. That's when silver goes to those "undreamed of heights" and it would take a lot for us to sell our hoard when the ship is sinking. Think about that for a second. What would cause you to sell your silver if you saw everything around you financially messed up? Most investors will only sell when they need to raise some cash for purchases.

Premiums on Silver for the Most Popular Bullion Products

I'll list below the lowest premium to highest premium products for silver.

1,000-ounce silver bars - these are bars that aren't exactly 1000 ounces but a range of 10% above or 10% below 1000 ounces as each bar is not made identically the same. They are just too big to get an exact weight each time. The 1,000-ounce bars are perfect for those who can buy them for their IRA as a trade as they can sell them with just a phone call at some point in the future. There is no cost for delivery of the metals to your IRA and the storage fees are minimal, especially when compared to the profit potential, plus the fact you don't have a bank in control of your wealth.

These bars offer the lowest spread and are not recommended for home delivery because of the weight where the bars are typically around 70lbs each. Also, the shipping costs to send it back are high and lugging it to the post office can be a pain. The downside is you can't break it in half or sell off chunks if you needed just a little bit of money for something and this was all you had to sell. You would have to sell the entire bar. That's why I recommend some coins in your IRA for liquidity purposes. But these large bars can be sent to and from the IRA custodian's depository free of charge.

100-ounce silver bars – these are popular for IRA's too and for taking delivery at home. 5 one hundred-ounce bars would weight about 31 lbs. They can be sold off a bar at a time in the future if you want to cost average out of a position or need to raise cash.

1-ounce Silver Rounds – .999 pure silver - These are my favorite coin for buying as they are low cost and fully liquid and could be used for barter if necessary. They have the same exact silver in them as American Eagles and Canadian Maple Leaf's, so why pay more for your silver for one of those government minted coins?

Junk Silver

Junk US 90% silver coins—often called "junk bags" — Were minted before 1965 and are a popular way to buy silver bullion. A full bag ($1,000 face amount of pre-1965 quarters, dimes or a mixture of both) contains approximately 715 ounces of "settled" silver and generally tracks the spot price of silver. These are circulated dimes and quarters that were used by citizens until the government found the silver content to be worth more than the price on the coins and stopped producing them since citizens were hoarding them (and still are).

The premiums on these will jump around as at times the bags disappear from existence as they don't make them any longer. From personal experience, rarely do I find those who buy these coins sell them back to us because investors view them as a great barter coin. It is easily recognizable and once was actual U.S. currency. They can be bought in sizes of $100 face value, all the way up to $1,000. A $1,000 face value bag weighs about 54lbs. You can always order two ½ bags at 27 pounds each if your back can't take the heavier weight. It's understood and the same price.

10-ounce silver bars – These are priced well too and are nice to look at. These can be used for barter as well.

Canadian Maple Leaf 1-ounce Silver Coin

.999 pure silver – These are popular with many because they want a government coin and it's cheaper than the U.S. coins. They are more expensive than one-ounce rounds, but the buyback is typically above spot for them. There is no guarantee it will always be this way however. I would rather as an investor have more silver for my money and pay less for it. That way I have more money in silver to sell when it comes time to take profit.

American Eagle 1-ounce Silver Coin

.999 pure silver – These coins are the most popular in the U.S. as they are American made and U.S. Mint produced. They are a beautiful coin. But you are paying for that beauty. They are more expensive than one-ounce rounds and Canadian Maples, but the buyback is typically higher above spot for them as with the Canadian coins (typically cost more to buy and pay more to you when sold). But again, there is no guarantee this will always be this way.

My Recommendation for Physical Delivery – Silver Rounds and 90% Junk Silver

My recommendation for physical delivery would be the silver rounds and if the premium is low, the 90% junk bags of silver. These coins are easier to transact with than large bars. Everyone should possess some of these coins as their base investment in silver.

CHAPTER 19

How to Profit by Investing in Silver

From 1970 to 1980, silver rose from about $2 to over $50. Granted, some of this rise was related to the Hunt Brothers' manipulation of the silver market, where they tried to—and did—corner the market by obtaining as much silver as they could, thus driving prices higher. The rules were changed to prevent this from occurring again and the Hunt brothers were convicted of conspiring to manipulate the market.

But at the same time of this move higher in the price of silver during the inflationary episode of the 70's, copper rose from 53 cents in 1970 to a high of $1.06 in 1979, platinum rose from $90 to $1,000 and agricultural commodities tripled.[1] I discuss how you can profit from many of these alternative investments in my Illusions of Wealth book,

Silver is a good investment because it is an industrial metal with many uses, as was discussed earlier, but also because it is viewed as a monetary metal. The simple fact that it has behaved inversely to the U.S. dollar over time, unlike that 1965 quarter. This shows that despite the many years of U.S. government intervention, silver is still viewed as a monetary safe-haven alternative to the U.S. dollar backed by basically nothing.

Silver has maintained the same pattern as gold over time in relation to also being a stable investment to counteract the U.S. dollar decline. At times silver is better investment than the dollar and at times the dollar better than silver, however over time silver has been shown to buy more and more and the dollar less and less. And let's not forget about the ever-increasing National Debt. Silver will always know what the debt situation is and what the sentiment is for it.

---

[1] The Hunt Brothers and the Silver Bubble, Brian Trumbore, President/Editor, StocksandNews.com

Silver Trading

Knowing when silver is overbought and oversold through sources like the Commitment of Traders and the gold/silver ratio is valuable information.[2] The COT data will give the trader insight as to whether large and small speculators are collectively long or short in the market, as well as what industry hedgers are up to. This is true for gold as well. This data typically comes out every Friday and smart money typically follows what the banks are doing. Dumb money what the funds are doing.

Seasonality: A Time to Go Long or Short for Traders

Seasonality is an important part of trading silver and gold. Historically, prices have risen during the last three months of the year and into the first five months of the following year, while the summer months have seen silver prices decline. Whether it is people doing other things, like taking vacations, investment demand decreases during the summer months.

Knowing this, a trader can be a little biased in trading the direction. The following chart shows the 40-year and 15-year seasonal pattern, followed by a chart of the 2000-2009 pattern showing the summer historic summer doldrums for silver. This is a pattern that has been consistent and one a trader can profit from utilizing. As the economy deteriorates, however, this pattern could become less reliable as silver garners more strength the full year rather than taking the summer off.

---

[2] Commitment of Traders Report Summary—Silver
http://www.technicalindicators.com/silvcotreport.htm

Buy Gold and Silver Safely

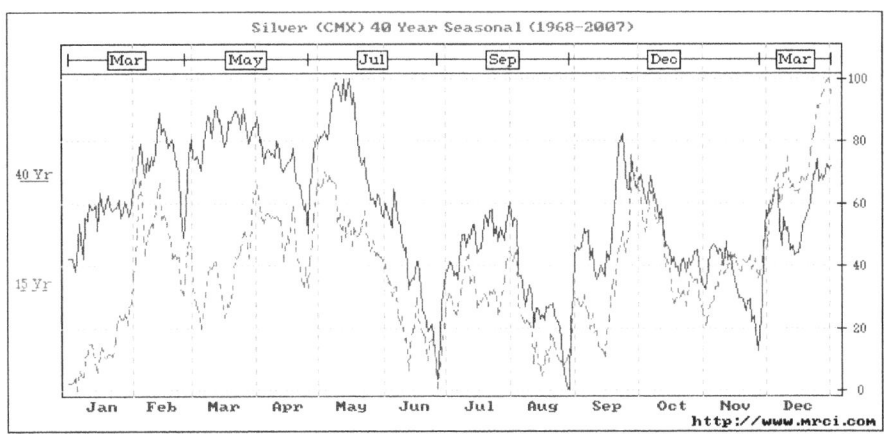

Year	Summer Low*	Date	Fall High**	Date	Gain
2001	$265.10	6-Jul	$293.25	17-Sep	10.6%
2002	$302.25	1-Aug	$349.30	27-Dec	15.6%
2003	$342.50	17-Jun	$416.25	31-Dec	21.5%
2004	$384.85	11-Jun	$454.20	2-Dec	18.0%
2005	$415.35	1-Jun	$536.50	12-Dec	29.2%
2006	$567.00	20-Jun	$648.75	1-Dec	14.4%
2007	$642.10	27-Jun	$841.10	8-Nov	31.0%
2008	$786.50	15-Aug	$905.00	29-Sep	15.1%
2009	$908.50	13-Jul	$1,212.50	2-Dec	33.5%
2010	$1,203.50	4-Jun	$1,421.00	9-Nov	18.1%
2011	$1,483.00	1-Jul	$1,895.00	5-Sep	27.8%
2012	$1,556.25	12-Jul	$1,791.75	4-Oct	15.1%
2013	$1,192.00	28-Jun	$1,399.50	3-Sep	17.4%
2014	$1,242.75	3-Jun	$1,286.50	1-Sep	3.5%
2015	$1,080.80	24-Jul	$1,184.25	15-Oct	9.6%
2016	$1,212.40	2-Jun	$1,348.35	7-Sep	11.2%
2017	$1211.90	7/11	$1291.85	11/28	6.60%

AVERAGE RETURN ABOUT 18%

---

[3] https://goldsilver.com/blog/the-best-time-to-buy-gold-and-silver-in-2017-is-in-2016/

Can Silver Be Manipulated?

In 1979, as mentioned earlier, the Hunt Brothers manipulated the silver market. The rules were changed to prevent such from occurring again, but there are some who think this manipulation continues today. They say the amount of silver traded on the exchange daily couldn't all be accounted for if just a few large traders demanded delivery. In other words, they trade in paper much more silver than exists.

Whether silver is manipulated or not, the price keeps going higher over time and especially when we all know what's next for the government in paying its bills once interest rates shoot higher. There will be no stopping silver, even with the attempts to counteract its move by the real manipulators: Congress, the Federal Reserve, and their banking buddies on Wall Street. Owning silver gives one some peace of mind no matter what happens in the future to our money.

The Nuts and Bolts of Investing in Silver – You Are No Longer an Average Investor

According to John Embry, Chief Investment Strategist, Sprott Asset Management, "The average retail investor has little or no investment in gold, and no understanding of how important it will be. An explosion in gold and silver is inevitable in the years to come."[4]

---

[4] John Embry, Chief Investment Strategist, Sprott Asset Management

CONCLUSION

What Percentage of Your Portfolio Needs to Be Protected with Gold and Silver?

The allocation into gold and silver should be approximately in the 10% to 20% range for your portfolio. The world over gold may be more popular than silver, as all central banks own gold and not silver, but one can look at the price historically and judge which investment may be better suited for them based on their timeframe to invest and acceptance of the risk involved with each. Silver is more volatile and gold the more conservative approach to investing. So, if you are older, your portfolio should be shifted more towards gold as it is more stable than silver. If you are younger, then more money should be put towards silver. But look again at the gold/silver ratio and make your buys according to it.

If you analyze the numbers like an engineer, if just 1% of the market value of the nation's publicly-traded shares (over $20 trillion), a total of $200 billion, was allocated to silver by investors, it would dwarf the number of ounces produced by gold and silver mines each year. This would naturally create a huge upward price movement in silver. What would be the catalyst? This entire book gave you the catalysts and they all center around one thing; governments can't control themselves and will always print more money and reduce the value of their currencies to the point of collapse.

This fiat money from around the world, that has unlimited printing presses behind it, will be chasing the real wealth of gold and silver in the years ahead.

My recommendations would be if conservative, a 75% allocation into gold and 25% into silver and if moderate, 50/50 and if aggressive, 75% silver and 25% gold. As these allocations go up in value, and they will over time, then you can shift to a more conservative approach with more put into gold. But keep in mind one thing; all the explaining in the world that I have tried to do in this book won't get you to pick up the phone and buy low. As the price of gold and silver move up and the reality of our economic and monetary system sets in, you'll either be glad you bought or wish you did.

Recap of Gold and Silver Recommendations

	Gold	**Silver**
Portfolio Allocation (10% - 20%)	75% (of allocation total) if conservative 50% (of allocation total) if moderate 25% (of allocation total) if aggressive	25% (of allocation total) if conservative 50% (of allocation total if) if moderate 25% (of allocation total) if aggressive
Coins for Delivery	1-ounce gold bars	1-ounce silver rounds, 10-ounce silver bars and 100-ounce silver bars
IRA, 401(k), SEP, Other Qualified Plans	1-ounce gold bars, 10-ounce gold bars, Kilo bars	100 and 1,000-ounce Bars but if you want liquidity, 1-ounce silver rounds

The Future

Once mutual fund managers, Certified Financial Planners and other financial advisors finally learn that gold and silver are the only real assets that counteract the fall or default of the U.S. dollar, millions upon millions of people will diversify by allocating a percentage to their portfolio.

Gold is the anchor that keeps your portfolio stabilized, and silver is the lifejacket to buoy your portfolio in the rough waters ahead.

As our Congress continues to spend, the credit contraction continues to implode down Exter's liquidity pyramid and the Federal Reserve continues to destroy its own balance sheet, you can bet more will wake up to the benefits that diversifying into gold and silver can bring.

If you liked this book and found value, please do us a favor and rate and add your comments on Amazon.com. It would be greatly appreciated.

Thank you for reading!

Keep up with the Current Thoughts on the precious metals markets;
http://buygoldandsilversafely.com/category/current-thoughts

Our store to purchase metals online is:
http://store.buygoldandsilversafely.com/

For those interested in purchasing any of the gold and silver coins and bars I recommended in this book, please contact us via one of the following:

Toll Free Number 888-604-6534
Outside of U.S. 619-500-8181
Email: info@buygoldandsilversafely.com

Online Store for Purchase of bullion Gold and Silver coins and bars from us; http://store.buygoldandsilversafely.com/ *Minimum investment is $1,500*

Buy Gold and Silver Safely Blog:
Articles written by Doug Eberhardt
http://www.buygoldandsilversafely.com/blog

Follow Doug Eberhardt and Buy Gold and Silver Safely:

Facebook
http://www.facebook.com/BuyGoldandSilver

Twitter
http://twitter.com/dougeberhardt

LinkedIn
http://www.linkedin.com/in/dougeberhardt

Debits & Credits

GLOSSARY

For many technical investment terminologies, I recommend you use Investopedia.com as a place to do your research.

Collateralized debt obligation - CDO: An investment-grade security backed by a pool of bonds, loans and other assets. CDOs do not specialize in one type of debt but are often non-mortgage loans or bonds. CDOs are unique in that they represent different types of debt and credit risk. In the case of CDOs, these different types of debt are often referred to as "tranches" or "slices.". Each slice has a different maturity and risk associated with it. The higher the risk, the more the CDO pays.

http://www.investopedia.com/terms/c/cdo.asp

Covered Bond: Covered bonds are debt instruments secured by a cover pool of mortgage loans (property as collateral) or public-sector debt to which investors have a preferential claim in the event of default. The issuance of covered bonds enables credit institutions to obtain lower cost of funding in order to grant mortgage loans for housing and non-residential property.

http://ecbc.hypo.org/content/default.asp?PageID=311

Credit Contraction: is a reaction to the unsustainable excesses of an inflationary credit expansion. During a deflationary credit contraction, capital, both real and fictitious, burrow down the liquidity pyramid, seeking safety and liquidity.

The Great Credit Contraction, Trace Mayer J.D. http://TheGreatCreditContraction.com

Credit Default Swap (CDS): is a contract where the buyer is entitled to payment from the seller of the CDS if there is a default by a particular company.

Credit Derivative: A financial contract that allows a party to take or reduce credit exposure generally on a bond, loan or index.

Credit Expansion: occurs when general market sentiment is moving capital, both real and fictitious, up the liquidity pyramid into less safe and less liquid assets. This results in the creation of "fictitious capital," which in turn results in inflated but illusory asset prices (the liquidity pyramid is discussed in the Credit Contraction section of this chapter).

The Great Credit Contraction, Trace Mayer J.D. http://TheGreatCreditContraction.com

Depression: A severe and prolonged recession characterized by inefficient economic productivity, high unemployment and falling price levels. In times of depression, consumers' confidence and investments decrease, causing the economy to shut down.

Deflation: Three Types

1. The first type consists of policies adopted by public authorities to deliberately reduce the quantity of money in circulation. This whole process of deliberate deflation contributes nothing and merely subjects the economic system to unnecessary pressure.

2. The second type of deflation, which should be clearly distinguished from the first, occurs when economic agents decide to save; that is, to refrain from consuming a significant portion of their income and to devote all or part of the monetary total saved to increasing their cash balances (i.e., to hoarding). In this case, the rise in the demand for money tends to push up the purchasing power of the monetary unit.

3. The third type of deflation we will consider results from the tightening of credit which normally occurs in the crisis and recession stage that follows all credit expansion. Just as credit expansion increases the quantity of money in circulation, the massive repayment of loans and the loss of value on the assets side of banks' balance sheets, both caused by the crisis, trigger

an inevitable, cumulative process of credit tightening which reduces the quantity of money in circulation and thus generates deflation. This third type of deflation arises when, as the crisis is emerging, not only does credit expansion stop increasing, but there is actually a credit squeeze and thus, deflation, or a drop in the money supply, or quantity of money in circulation.

PP. 445-448, 452-453 Money, Bank Credit, and Economic Cycles, Jesús Huerta de Soto, 2006

Derivative: A financial contract whose value is derived from the performance of underlying market factors, such as interest rates, currency exchange rates, commodity, credit, financial indexes and equity prices. Derivative transactions include a wide assortment of financial contracts, including structured debt obligations and deposits, swaps, futures, options, caps, floors, collars, forwards and various combinations thereof.

http://www.occ.treas.gov/ftp/release/2010-71a.pdf

Fiat Money: i.e. Federal Reserve Notes – Currency that a government has declared to be legal tender, despite the fact that it has no intrinsic value and is not backed by reserves. Historically, most currencies were based on physical commodities such as gold or silver, but fiat money is based solely on faith. Most of the world's paper money is fiat money. Because fiat money is not linked to physical reserves, it risks becoming worthless due to hyperinflation. If people lose faith in a nation's paper currency, the money will no longer hold any value.

http://www.investopedia.com/terms/f/fiatmoney.asp

Flow of Funds: A set of accounts that is used to follow the flow of money within various sectors of an economy. Specifically, the account analyzes economic data on borrowing, lending and investment throughout sectors like households, businesses and farms. The data from the FOF accounts can be compared to prior data to analyze the financial strength of the economy at a certain time and to see where the economy may go in the future. The accounts can also be used by governments to formulate monetary and fiscal policy.

http://www.investopedia.com/terms/f/fof.asp

Fractional Reserve Banking: A practice in which banks keep only a fraction of their deposits in reserve (as cash and other highly liquid assets) and lend out the remainder, while maintaining the simultaneous obligation to redeem all deposits immediately upon demand.

The Great Credit Contraction, Trace Mayer, J.D. http://TheGreatCreditContraction.com

GDP: The monetary value of all finished goods and services within a country's borders in a specific time period. It includes all private and public consumption, government outlays, investments and exports less imports that occur within a defined territory. (Explained in detail in Chapter 1.)

Farlex Financial Dictionary   http://financial-dictionary.thefreedictionary.com/Per+capita+GDP

Hyperinflation: Extremely rapid or out-of-control inflation. When associated with depressions, hyperinflation often occurs when there is a large increase in the money supply not supported by gross domestic product (GDP) growth, resulting in an imbalance in the supply and demand for the money.

http://www.investopedia.com/terms/h/hyperinflation.asp

Inflation: is an increase in the supply of money and credit relative to available goods and services.

Stoneleigh: The Automatic Earth -

http://theautomaticearth.blogspot.com/2009/07/july-5-2009-unbearable-mightiness-of.html

Money Supply: Beyond the scope of a Glossary definition. See Michael Pollaro's Austrian take at http://mises.org/daily/4297 and http://trueslant.com/michaelpollaro/austrian-money-supply/ for a more detailed explanation.

Monetizing the Debt: The Fed would effectively be financing deficit spending by "printing" money. It would simply be a two-step process: The government would sell debt to the public and the Fed would exchange the public's holdings of government debt for money. The Federal Reserve's definition: the goal of the Fed, and most other central banks, is to promote maximum sustainable economic growth and price stability. In the process of achieving this goal, the money supply expands over time with the needs of a growing economy. While the Fed's actions to increase the supply of money over time would, in effect, be financing deficit spending by "printing" money, this would not be the purpose of the Fed's actions and, hence, critics would be wrong to claim that the Fed has monetized the debt. I suggest that an economically meaningful definition of "monetizing the debt" must be based on the Fed's motive for increasing the money supply.

Economic Synopses: Short essays and reports on the economic issues of the day, 2010, Number 14, "Monetizing the Debt." http://research.stlouisfed.org/publications/es/10/ES1014.pdf

Paper Money: Bank notes designated by the U.S. Treasury as legal tender for payment of debts, principally Federal Reserve Notes. Paper money is also known as fiat money because it is not backed by the issuing government's pledge to exchange paper for an equivalent amount of gold or hard currency.

http://www.allbusiness.com/glossaries/paper-money/4946142-1.html

Recession: A significant decline in activity across the economy, lasting longer than a few months. It is visible in industrial production, employment, real income and wholesale-retail trade.

http://www.investopedia.com/terms/r/recession.asp

Spread: The dollar amount one pays over the spot price of gold. Gold dealer costs are typically around 3% and will charge an amount above this 3% to encompass the entire spread one pays.

Unemployment: is often used as a measure of the health of the economy. The most frequently cited measure of unemployment is the unemployment rate. This is the number of unemployed persons divided by the number of people in the labor force. Many different variations of the unemployment rate exist with different definitions concerning who is an "unemployed person" and who is in the "labor force." For example, the U.S. Bureau of Labor Statistics commonly cites the "U-3" unemployment rate as the official unemployment rate but this definition of unemployment does not include unemployed workers who have become discouraged by a tough labor market and are no longer looking for work.

http://www.investopedia.com/terms/u/unemployment.asp

Velocity of Money: the rate at which money changes hands. It is *psychological* factors — desire to buy and sell, produce and consume — that determine velocity.[132]1 If we increase the supply of money and velocity stays the same, if GDP does not grow, it means we'll have inflation, because this equation must balance. But if you reduce velocity (which is happening today), and if you don't increase the supply of money, you are going to see deflation.[133]

---

[132] The Velocity of Circulation: Mises Daily, March 17, 2008, Henry Hazlitt
[133] The Trend May Not Be Your Friend, John Mauldin, April 18, 2009

Index

A

AARP magazine, 144
allocations, typical asset, 11
American Buffalo Gold Coin, 96
American Eagle 1-ounce bullion coins, 122
American Eagle 1-ounce Silver Coin, 172
American Eagle Bullion Coins, 94
American Eagle Gold Bullion Coin, 95
American Eagle Gold Coin, 96
American Eagles, 95, 117–19, 128, 159, 171
   one-ounce gold, 132
American Gold Buffalo, 95–96
American Gold Eagle, 27, 95, 97
America's Great Depression, 61, 66
AMEX Gold Miners index, 101
Analysis of Stocks, 84
Anti Money Laundering activities, 131
APMEX Buy Price, 120
Armageddon, 76–77
asset allocation, 11, 26
asset allocation models, 14, 75, 79
assets
   risk-free, 31
   riskiest, 64
Austrian School of Economic Thought, 40

B

Baby Boomer, 162
   first, 161–62
bags, junk, 171–72
balance sheet recession, 65

Baltic Dry Index Chart, 70
Baltic Dry Sea Index, 70
bank holiday, 134
banking, fractional reserve, 37, 39, 186
banking crisis, 72, 74
banking system, 9, 72
bankruptcies, 6, 9, 39, 46, 52, 73, 82, 91
bankruptcy laws, 46
banks, 16, 19–20, 37–39, 46, 48, 53–54, 58, 60–61, 72–74, 83–84, 86, 99–100, 134–37, 150–51, 164–65
  central, xii–xiii, 1, 17, 19–20, 80, 83, 97, 159, 178, 187
  commercial, 72, 154
Barrick Gold, 102
bars
  1,000-ounce, 170, 179
  1-ounce, 97
  10-ounce, 132
  100-ouncesilver, 171
  1000-ounce, 130
  bullion, 28
barter, 77, 95, 171–72
BBB (Better Business Bureau), 109, 139
Beck, Glenn, 112, 115, 122–23
Bernanke, 46
bitcoins, xiii, 83, 87, 108
Bretton Woods, 17
Bretton Woods system, 17
Brief History of Gold and Federal Reserve Notes, 16
Brinks, 140
British Pound, 24
bullion, 113, 124, 128, 146, 152
bullion coins, 113, 115, 117–18, 122, 125, 146
  1-ounce gold, 95
bullion coins and bars, 93, 113, 125, 146
business cycle, 39–40
business spending, 3

Bust Cycles, 85
buyback, 120, 172
buyers of gold, 84, 112
Buy Gold and Silver Safely Blog, 180
Buying Gold Investment Grid, 126

C

California Gold Rush, 21
Canadian coins, 172
Canadian Maple Leaf, 27, 95, 124, 132, 171
Canadian Maple Leaf 1-ounce Silver Coin, 172
cash transactions, 131
CDOs, 183
CDs, 7, 14, 18, 91, 183
Central bankers, 83
Central Bank Gold Agreement, 19–20
Central Bank Sales Agreements, 21
CFP (Certified Financial Planners), xii, 27, 179
CFP investment book, 28
CFTC (Commodity Futures Trading Commission), 109, 111, 128, 130
CFTC-approved contracts for gold coins, 129
CFTC-approved RFC, 129
Chairman Janet Yellen, 46
China, 7, 9, 14, 39, 156, 158
China exchange, 7
Chinese Gold Panda, 95
Christ, Jesus, 16
Christian, Jeffrey, 155–56
circulation, quantity of money in, 59–60, 184–85
clients, gold dealer's rip-off, 144
Closed-End Funds, 106
CME, 108
CNBC, xiii, 24, 53
CNBC commentators, xii–xiii
CNBC journalist Melissa Lee, 41

Code of Federal Regulations, 118
Coinage Act, 150
Coin Facts for Investors, 123
coins
  1.5-ounce, 121, 143
  1.5-ounce silver Polar Bear, 120
  1-ounce, 94–95, 154
  barter, 171
  high commission, 122
  one-ounce gold Canadian Maple Leaf, 132
  pre-1933, 117
  proof, 138, 143–44
  semi-numismatic, 124
Coins & Bars, 157
Collateralized debt obligation, 183
COMEX market, 97
commissions, 30, 101, 110, 113, 117
  high, xiv, 11, 124, 169
Commitment of Traders, 174
Committee on Banking and Currency, 153
commodities, 2, 11, 26, 185
  agricultural, 173
  physical, 185
Commodity Futures Trading Commission. *See* CFTC
Common Objections, 75
confiscation, 16, 107, 116, 118
confiscation of gold, 16, 95, 117–18
confiscation ploy, 116
Congress, xi–xii, 4, 6–7, 33–34, 39, 52–55, 59–61, 72–74, 81, 83, 126, 128, 151–53, 176, 179
Congressional spending, 9
Constitution, 56, 71, 149, 151, 154
consumer demand, 128
Consumer Protection Act, 72
Consumer Reports search, 123
consumer spending, 3, 45

copper, 95, 150, 173
COT data, 174
counterfeit, 96–97
counterfeiting, 96
CPI, 33
CPM Group's Silver Yearbook, 155
credit card debt, 47
credit card delinquencies, 74
credit contraction, 9, 39, 59, 61, 91, 179, 183–84, 186
credit contraction and deflation, 9, 58
Credit Default Swap, 183
Credit Derivative, 183
credit expansion, 39, 60, 184
    inflationary, 37, 183
Credit Expansion and Inflation, 37
Credit Suisse and PAMP gold bars, 97
crisis, 32, 34, 53, 59–60, 84, 125, 184–85
cryptocurrencies, xiii, 64, 108
    trading/storing, 108
cycles, 14, 39, 43, 46, 54, 75, 83, 86, 102

D

debt-based economy, 35
debt ceiling, 4, 6, 54, 82
debt deflation, 65
debt limit, xi, 6
DebtLimitUSA, 6
debts, bad, 60
Debt-to-GDP ratio, 61
deficit spending, financing, 186–87
deflation, 9, 39, 58–61, 64, 66, 72, 81, 91, 184–85
deflationary contraction, 68, 87, 92
deflationary credit contraction, 60–61, 64, 70, 85, 183
Deflationary Credit Contraction Unfolds, 34
deflationary trends, 80

Deflation First, 59
delivery, 90, 97–99, 106, 111, 129, 140, 144, 160, 170, 179
  taking, 90, 106, 140, 169, 171
depressions, 40, 184, 186
diversification, 25, 30, 83, 85, 87, 149
diversified allocation Charles Schwab, 12
diversified portfolio, 13, 26–27, 33, 80
Dodd Frank Wall Street Reform, 72
dollar-based portfolio, 13, 111
dollar bill, 2, 6
dollar cost average approach, 138
Dollar Crash, 8
dollar currency risk, 15
dollar depreciation, 29, 93
dollar exposure, 25, 90
Dollar Index, 8, 87–88
dollar risk, 11, 14, 28, 30, 84
dollars, xi–xiii, 1–2, 5–8, 13–15, 17–21, 30–33, 75–77, 80–83, 87–88, 90–92, 111–13, 115–16, 125–26, 161–63, 173
  declining, 79, 165
  peace silver, 124
dollar value, 161
dollar weakness, 33
Dow/Gold Ratio, 89
Dow Jones Industrial Average, 77
Dow Theory Letters, 80

E

Eagles, 96, 132, 137
Early Release Scam, 118
economic cycles, 34, 185
economic issues, 187
economics, 30, 34, 84, 86
Economic Thought, 40
Economist John Exter, 32, 74

economists, 34, 36, 42, 64
  mainstream, 35
economy, 2–3, 5, 9–10, 32–33, 35, 39–43, 45–46, 51–52, 59–60, 65–66, 81–82, 86, 137, 184–85, 187
  frail, 114
economy deflates, 86
estate, real, 33, 40, 68, 76, 79, 82–83
ETFs (Exchange Traded Funds), 12, 21, 32, 91, 93, 98–101, 104, 145, 160–61
Euro, 8, 19–20, 24, 32, 75, 87
European coins, 115–17
European gold coins, 124
executive orders, 117–18
  revoked, 118
Exempting Pre-1933 Gold Coins, 118
Exter, 18
  John, 18, 64
Exter's Pyramid, 43, 92
Exter's son-in-law Barry Downs, 18

F

FANG stocks, 42
FDIC, 48, 134–35
FDIC guidelines, 135
Federal Reserve, xii, 1–2, 5, 18, 20, 30, 32, 34, 38–40, 46, 53–54, 60, 72, 74, 153
Federal Reserve Act, 6, 16, 152
Federal Reserve Banks, 2, 6
Federal Reserve intervention, 34
Federal Reserve policy, 93
Federal Reserve's definition, 187
Federal Reserve System, xiii, 35, 54, 74
fees, 99, 101, 109, 123–25, 140
  storage, 106, 108, 170
fiat currencies, 161

financial advisors, xii, 10–11, 19, 25–27, 29–30, 34, 52, 100, 112, 114, 179
financial crisis, 30, 46, 61, 77, 86
financial media, 8, 53, 55, 67, 88, 149
financial planning, 27, 164
Financial Risk, 25
First Strike coins, 119
foreign markets, 14
founding fathers, 71, 149
fraud, 100, 140
French francs, 115
FRNs (Federal Reserve Notes), 1–2, 5–7, 9, 16–17, 29, 77, 81, 107, 152–54, 185, 187

G

GDP (gross domestic product), 2–3, 5–6, 9, 40–42, 45, 66, 70, 86, 186
GDP, 2018's, 41
GDP growth, 9, 45
GDP ratio, 66
GDX, 91, 101
GDXJ, 91, 101, 104
GLD, 21, 98
GLD Prospectus, 99–100
gold, xi–xiv, 1–5, 7, 9–11, 13–33, 35, 55, 69–71, 75–77, 79–91, 93–103, 105–19, 121–46, 149–55, 177–81
  bullion, 111, 117, 143–44, 146, 180
  confiscated, 107
  hedge, 91
  liquid, 131
  low commissioned, xiv
  paper, 101, 106
  private, 117
  purchase, 115, 138–40
gold and silver
  physical, 90–91, 94, 141, 145

price of, 113, 167, 178
Gold and Silver Recommendations, 179
gold bars, 97–98, 106, 126, 132, 137
　1-ounce, 142, 179
　10-ounce, 179
　allocated, 100
gold bugs, xiii, 8, 77
gold bullion, 111, 117
Gold Bullion Coin Act, 95, 128
gold bullion coins, 94, 117, 122, 128
Gold Certificates, 93, 106–7, 117
gold coins, 16–17, 94–95, 116–18, 124, 129, 132, 136–38
　1-ounce, 95
　physical, 93, 126
Gold Coin Sales, 127
gold dealer industry, 122
gold dealers, xiv, 7–8, 11, 28, 94, 97–98, 109–20, 122, 124–25, 131, 139–44, 169
Gold-dealers, 11
Gold Dealer Sales Tactics, 116
Gold Dealers' Tactics, 114
gold ETF, popular, 98
gold funds, 101
Gold Futures, 130
gold holdings, 102, 135
gold insurance, 51
Gold Investment Grid, 127
gold investments, 83, 91, 93, 97, 109, 115
　popular, 132
gold investors, 77
Goldline, 123–24
Goldline International, 112, 122
Goldline's rebuttal, 123
Goldman Sachs, 73, 85
Gold Miners ETF, 101
Gold Miners ETF Prospectus, 101

gold mining companies, 101
Gold Mining ETFs, 93, 101
gold-mining stocks, 91, 98, 101, 103, 106
Gold Mining Stocks, 102
Goldmoney, 108
Goldmoney Inc, xiii, 93, 108
gold one-ounce bars, 132
gold ownership, 133
Gold prices, 19, 23, 55
gold rush, 127
gold salesman, 114–15
gold/silver ratio, 143, 167–68, 174, 178
  monthly, 167
Gold Standard Act, 151
GoldStar Trust, 141
Good Inflation Hedge, 75
government bonds, 11–12
government confiscation, 116
government-manipulated CPI figures, 33
government shutdowns, 126
government spending, xii, 3–6, 45, 52
  unprecedented, 19
GPS (Global Positioning Satellite), 134
Great Depression, 39, 43, 61, 66
Greece, 22, 77
growth, real, 57

H

Hayek, 24
hedge funds, 84
higher-taxes-or-higher-inflation, 41
Historical ratios of gold and silver, 167
hoarding, 59, 171, 184
home delivery, 170
housing boom, 86

housing bubble, 46
HUI Index, 91, 102
Hunt Brothers, 173, 176
Hunt Brothers' manipulation, 173
hyperinflation, 72, 185–86

I

IAU, 98–99
Index Fund, 30
industrial applications, 155, 157
industries, financial services, 10, 25, 27–28, 114
inflation, xi–xiii, 5, 7, 9, 13, 18, 30, 33, 37, 39, 46, 58–60, 85, 88, 115–16
  super, xii, 85
inflation hedge, 75
inflation rates, 17–18, 60
infrastructure, 45
insurance companies, 137
interest rates, xi, 3, 29, 32, 39, 74, 81, 86, 91, 185
  higher, 18, 32
  low, 87
Investing in gold-mining stocks, 101
investment demand, 157–58, 161, 174
investment pyramid, 25–26, 28
Investment Pyramid Flaw, 26
investments, xi, 26–27, 29–30, 39–40, 46, 76–77, 84, 88, 90–91, 102–3, 106–7, 109–11, 173, 177–78, 184–86
  good, 26–27, 173
  lousy, 77
  stable, 173
investment strategies, xi, 35
investor portfolios, 11, 29
investors
  aggressive, 91, 102, 104, 110
  conservative, 90–91

prudent, 29
IRA, 83, 140–45, 170–71, 179
  self-directed, 141
IRA investor, 141
IRA rollover, 141
IRA transfer, 141
IRS, 107, 116, 128, 131
Ishares Comex Gold Trust, 98

J

Jackson, Andrew, 151
Japan, 7, 9, 14, 39, 61–62, 66, 86, 91
Japanese Yen, 24
Japan's GDP, 61
Junior Gold Miners ETF, 101
Junk bonds, 91
Junk Silver, 171–72

K

Keynesian economists, 34, 39
Kilo bars, 142, 179

L

legal tender, 2
Legal Tender for Eagles, 137
lending, fractional-reserve, 72
leverage, 67, 109–10
Leveraging, 93, 109
liquidity, 64, 131, 179, 183
liquidity pyramid, 183–84
  down Exter's, 179
loans, student, 49
local coin shop, 138

Longer-Term Treasuries, 164
low inflation, 57

M

manipulation, 160, 176
market conditions, 124
market sentiment, 85, 184
market turmoil, 127
Market Vectors Junior Gold Miners Index, 101
melt value, actual, 35
metal ownership, 108
millennials, 51
Minimum Reportable Amount, 131
Modern Portfolio Theory. *See* MPT
monetary crisis, 133
monetary history, 51
monetary policy, 4
monetary structure, 153
monetary system, 51, 72, 74, 87, 93–94
monetary value, 2, 153, 155, 186
Monex, 109
money, xii–xiii, 3–5, 24–25, 37–38, 51, 54–55, 59–60, 68–71, 74–77, 109–10, 124, 149–50, 152–53, 161–65, 184–87
  fiat, 152, 178, 185, 187
  lawful, 2, 7
  printed, 54
  real, 77, 81, 164
money markets, 7, 13, 18, 84
money orders, 140
money power, national banking, 151–52
money supply, 37, 39, 60, 72, 185–87
MPT (Modern Portfolio Theory), 25, 30–32
mutual funds, 12, 26, 84, 91, 99–101, 106, 145

N

national debt, xi, 3, 32, 40, 54–55, 61, 74
National Debt and gold, xi
New Direction, 141
NGC, 110, 118–19, 124
Nixon decoupling, 17
numismatic, 124
　high commissioned, 124
numismatic coins, 27, 93, 110, 114, 124–25
NYSE Arca Gold Miners, 101

O

Obama administration, 41
ownership, private, 17
owning gold, 126, 133

P

PAMP gold bars, 97
paper money, xi, 187
PCGS, 124
　recognized grading services, 110
pensions, 9, 68–69
Perth Mint, 107
Perth Mint Certificates, 107
physical gold, 9, 90–91, 93–94, 98, 100–102, 106, 108, 126, 141, 145
platinum, 108, 128, 173
Polar Bear & Cub 1.5-ounce silver coins, 120
policies
　fiscal, 185
　homeowner's, 137
Portfolio Allocation, 179
portfolio insurance, 83
precious metals, xiii–xiv, 27–28, 35, 79, 82, 107, 113, 128–29, 145, 149, 152–53, 155

precious metals IRA, 141
Premium Fluctuation, 169
premiums, 94, 110, 115, 128, 169–72
  higher, 132
  lowest, 170
President Trump, xi, 3–5, 46, 52, 82
prices, buyback, 115, 125, 131
printing money, 186–87
Producer Hedging, 160
Prudent Investor Rule, 28–29
prudent investor rule set, 29
Purchase of bullion Gold and Silver coins, 180
Purchase Physical Gold, 138
pyramid, 25, 64, 67, 70
Pyramid of Financial Risk, 25

Q

QE, 86
QE stimulus, 86–87
quarters, pre-1965, 171

R

rare coins, 110–11, 118, 122, 125
  selling high-priced, 111
rate hikes, 46
Real Estate Investment Trust (REITs), 11, 14
Real GDP, 40, 45
Recap of Gold and Silver, 179
recessions, 30, 32, 43, 46, 48, 65, 69, 74, 81, 187
  ordinary, 65
  prolonged, 184
regulated futures contract. *See* RFC
REITs (Real Estate Investment Trust), 11, 14
reporting requirements, 128, 131, 139

retirement, 12, 37, 68–70, 145
retirement planning, 9, 11
RFC (regulated futures contract), 128–30
RipoffReport.com, 139
risk free assets, 32, 88
risks
  higher, 28
  leverage, 110
RMC (Republic Metals Corporation), 97
Roman Empire, 16
Royal Canadian Mint (RCM), 97, 127
Russell, Richard, 80–82

S

safe deposit boxes, 134–36
Sales of precious metals, 128–29
self-directed IRA companies, 141
Sell Gold, 146
silver, xii–xiv, 1–2, 7, 9–11, 13–15, 35, 69–71, 90–91, 94–95, 113, 128–34, 136–38, 140–45, 149–74, 176–79
  physical, 90, 161, 169
  pure, 171–72
silver bars
  1,000-ounce, 170
  10-ounce, 172, 179
  100-ounce, 179
silver bullion, 113, 125, 144, 171
silver bullion coins, 119
silver certificates, 153–54
silver coins, 94–95, 131, 137, 141, 143, 154, 156, 169, 171, 180
  1.5-ounce, 143
silver content value, 111
silver dollar, 152
Silver ETFs, 101, 160
silver investments, 141, 143, 164, 169

silver market, 173, 176
silver prices, 156, 174
silver proof coins, 143
silver rounds, 172
  1-ounce, 142, 171, 179
Silver Supply, 158
Silver Usage and Mining data, 155
SLV, 161
Social Security, 33, 69, 81, 161–62
spot, 33, 94, 113, 119, 121, 132, 172
spot price, 94, 97, 115, 143, 169, 171
Sprott Asset Management, 177
Sprott Physical Gold Trust, 98
stock market conditions, 85
stock markets, xi, 12, 14, 17, 26–27, 37, 41, 69, 72, 74–75, 79, 81, 83–84, 89
Stocks & Mutual Funds, 93
storage, 108, 135
storage facility, 141
survival, 77, 133
Swiss 20-franc coin, 116
Swiss francs, 24, 115–16
system
  education, 21, 112
  financial, xiii, 85
Systematic Risk, 30

T

Tactical Asset Allocation, 85
taxes, 55, 69, 107, 141, 144, 153
  hidden, 5
Tocqueville Gold fund, 106
Total Credit Market Debt, 66
treasuries, 2, 5, 7, 9–10, 12, 32, 39, 64, 81, 91–92, 153–54, 187
  long-term, 164

Treasury Bonds, 31
Treasury Direct, 33
Treasury Inflation Protected Securities, 33
Treasury's definition of FRNs, 2
Trump, Donald, 4, 81–82
Trump effect, 45

U

unemployment rate, 57, 60, 187
Uniform Prudent Investor Act, 29
United States Mint, 94
United States Treasury, 2
US banks, 73

V

Valcambi, 97
Velocity of Money, 70
Volcker, 18–19
  Paul, 18

W

Wage Growth, 57
Walking Liberty, 124
wealth
  perceived, 161
  real, 83, 93, 111, 161, 178
WEF (World Economic Forum), 86
World Gold Council, 19–20
World Silver Survey, 158–59

X

Y

Yen/Dollar, 88

Z

Zimbabwe, 88
Zimbabwe's currency inflation, 88
zinc batteries, 156

Made in the USA
Las Vegas, NV
20 July 2022